STRONG GROUND

*Mount Independence and
the American Revolution*

STRONG GROUND

Mount Independence and the American Revolution

Donald H. Wickman and the Mount Independence Coalition

Original illustrations by Gary Zaboly

Published by the Mount Independence Coalition
Orwell, Vermont
2017

The mission of the Mount Independence Coalition is to support the efforts of the Vermont Division for Historic Preservation and the Mount Independence State Historic Site to protect and interpret a unique historic and natural treasure. Located in Orwell, Vermont, Mount Independence honors the sacrifice, the ingenuity and the courage of those who rallied to their nation's defense.

Edited by Ennis Duling & Stephen Zeoli.

Original illustrations edited by Ron Morgan.

Cover Art: Ernest Haas, *Mount Independence 1776-1777* / Mount Independence Coalition

© Copyright 2017 Donald H. Wickman and the Mount Independence Coalition
Orwell, Vermont

All rights reserved. No part of this book may be reproduced without
permission from the Mount Independence Coalition.

For more information visit: MountIndependence.org

Book Design: David Carlson, Carlson & Company, Inc. Middlebury, Vermont

Artifacts from the Collection of the Mount Independence Historic Site appear on pages
15, 18, 20, 30, 31, 42, 43, 60.

Photos by Ennis Duling appear on pages 23, 24, 44, 51, 61, 62, 72, 90, 91, 92, 93.

ISBN: 978-0-692-86228-5

Contents

	INTRODUCTION	1
CHAPTER ONE	General Philip Schuyler's Decision	4
	A beaten, smallpox-ridden army leaves Crown Point for Mount Independence	
CHAPTER TWO	Under the Direction of Jeduthan Baldwin	17
	A wooded peninsula becomes a major American fortification	
CHAPTER THREE	Mastery of the Lake	27
	At opposite ends of Lake Champlain, American and British forces prepare for battle	
CHAPTER FOUR	A Long, Bitter Winter	39
	Commander Anthony Wayne and 2,000 men suffer from disease and cold	
CHAPTER FIVE	Plans, Politics, and Preparations	47
	Jeduthan Baldwin begins construction on the Great Bridge, a hospital, and a fort	
CHAPTER SIX	General Arthur St. Clair's Predicament	57
	An unprepared, outnumbered garrison faces General John Burgoyne's confident invasion	
CHAPTER SEVEN	A Controversial Retreat	65
	With the Lake Champlain forts nearly surrounded, General St. Clair orders a retreat	
CHAPTER EIGHT	A British and German Post Under Siege	77
	While Burgoyne marches to defeat, Mount Independence withstands an American counterattack	
EPILOGUE	Recognition and Preservation	87
	Farmland becomes a Vermont State Historic Site	
	Glossary	94
	Recommended Reading and Sources	96
	Index	100
	About the Mount Independence Coalition	104

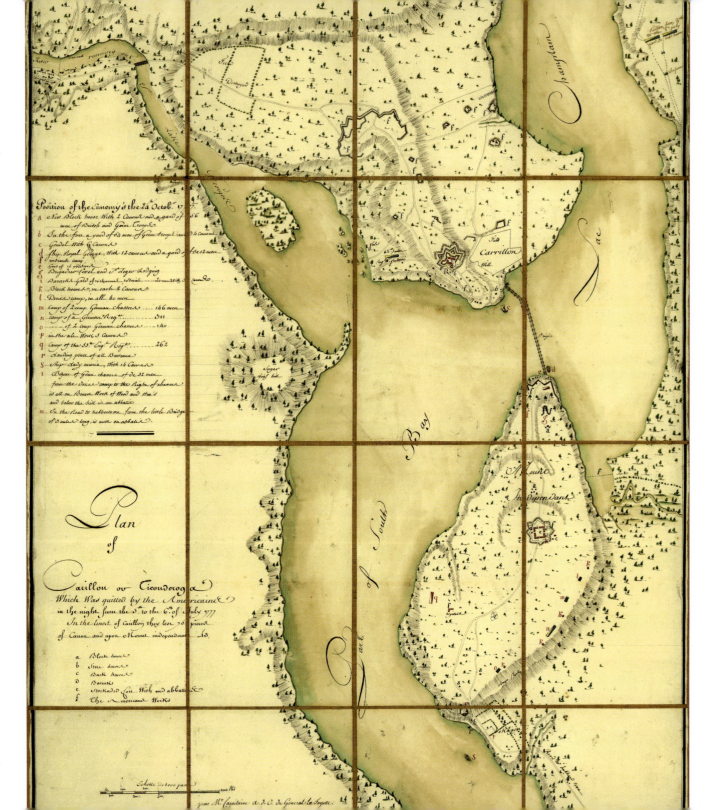

A map of Mount Independence and Ticonderoga drawn by Michel Capitaine de Chesnoy for the Marquis de Lafayette, who in the winter of 1778 commanded on the northern frontier from headquarters in Albany. Library of Congress

Preceding pages: Artist and historian Gary Zaboly imagines the view looking north from Mount Independence on October 28, 1776, which includes the extensive defenses of Ticonderoga on the western shore of Lake Champlain. A floating bridge is soon to be installed connecting the two posts. Gary Zaboly / Mount Independence Coalition

Introduction

From July 1776 into July 1777, the fate of the newly independent United States of America rested upon a rocky peninsula on the east side of Lake Champlain, located in today's Orwell, Vermont. Called at first East Point or Rattlesnake Hill, this strong defensive position was named Mount Independence after the Declaration of Independence was read to the assembled soldiers. The Americans on the Mount turned back a British invasion in the fall of 1776. Like the men at Valley Forge a year later, they suffered from cold and privation during a winter encampment. Then in July 1777, they saved themselves and their cause in a sudden, controversial retreat.

For four months in 1777, Mount Independence was occupied by German and British troops. They strengthened the fortifications and withstood an American counterattack as the bulk of the invading army under General John Burgoyne marched south to defeat at Bennington and surrender at Saratoga.

References to Mount Independence can be found in any good history of the American Revolution, but few historians have written about the Mount in its national context, and its story has been largely overshadowed by the compelling, but often-told story of Fort Ticonderoga. One purpose of *Strong Ground* is to bring the Mount to the forefront and to see the thousands of men encamped there as part of a crucial effort to defend northern New York, New England, and the cause of American liberty. The story of Mount Independence is one of hardship and enormous courage, and it lies at the heart of the struggle that was the American Revolution. Mount Independence is a national treasure, the least disturbed major military site associated with the birth of the nation.

Today Mount Independence is a Vermont State Historic Site, with a fine museum and more than six miles of hiking trails. The Mount is different from other historic fortifications in the Champlain Valley. Fort Ticonderoga is an early-twentieth-century reconstruction; massive Crown Point and its French predecessor, Fort

Saint-Frédéric, are impressive ruins; but Mount Independence, which was stripped of trees by 1777, has returned to nature. Along its forested trails, the earthen walls of the Citadel and the Grand Battery loom over the lake as they did in 1776-1777; the foundations of the General Hospital and the blockhouses built by American, British, and German troops still peek up from the surface to remind us of their former presence; the magnificent Southern Battery, designed by Polish military engineer Thaddeus Kosciuszko, who became an international hero, dominates a key vantage point; and a clearing where a star-shaped picket fort once stood beckons to the imagination, while many other intriguing features await the curious visitor.

For more than a decade, the Mount Independence Coalition—the friends group that supports the work of the historic site—has dreamed of a book about the Mount that enriches understanding and makes this special place come alive. *Strong Ground* introduces readers to the Mount's neglected but gripping story and we hope it inspires historians to delve deeper in their research.

Many people deserve our thanks.

For their vital historical insights and criticisms that made this book far more complete than it otherwise would have been…
Mike Barbieri
Alan Berolzheimer
The Fort Ticonderoga Association particularly Rich Strum,
    Chris Fox, and Stuart Lille
John W. Krueger
William Powers

Nothing happens around Mount Independence without the knowledge and efforts of regional site administrator Elsa Gilbertson and site interpreters Paul Andriscin, Maureen Bertrand, and Tobrina Calvin. The longtime trail crew of Steve Bird and Philip Keyes makes it possible to walk the trails and enjoy the grounds.

A German map of Mount Independence from the fall of 1777. Staatsarchiv Marburg

For their generous financial support...

Lee Allphin, Jr. and Gail Allphin
Judith M. Buechner
Ann Clay
John Dumville
Richard and Joyce Fifield
George H. Helmer
Mark D. Hill (From Charitable Trust)
Beverly Jacobson
Warren and Barry King
Bob Maguire
Ron R. Morgan
David C. Pinkham
Kurt and Victoria Singer
Harmon Thurston
Nicholas and Joanne Zeoli

Special gratitude to Dorothy Morgan

Strong Ground Book Committee

Paul Andriscin
Mark Brownell
Ennis Duling
Elsa Gilbertson
Donna Martin
R. Duncan Mathewson, III
Ron Morgan
Jim Ross
Rustan Swenson
Joe Taparauskas
Steve Zeoli

Mount Independence State Historic Site Administration

Tracy Martin, Historic Sites Section Chief
Elsa Gilbertson, Historic Sites Regional Administrator

Strong Ground is dedicated to the men and women —
American, British, and German —
who served on Mount Independence.

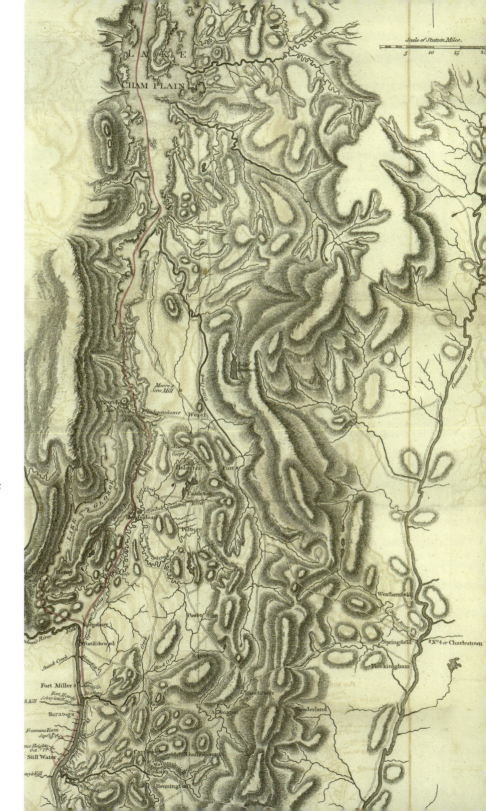

A map of General John Burgoyne's campaign in 1777. Engraved by William Faden / Collection of Mount Independence State Historic Site

The point of Mount Independence juts nearly due north into Lake Champlain. In the photo, East Creek is to left. To the right, Lake Champlain is a quarter-mile wide. Alan Nyiri photo

CHAPTER ONE

General Philip Schuyler's Decision

"The ground . . . we found so remarkably strong as to require little labour to make it tenable against a vast superiority of force, and fully to answer the purpose of preventing the enemy from penetrating into the country to the south of it."

— Philip Schuyler to George Washington, July 12, 1776

"Alas! what will become of our distressed army, Death reigns triumphant," Dr. Lewis Beebe reported from Crown Point in his journal for June 29, 1776. Beebe was serving with Colonel Charles Burrall's Connecticut State Regiment, which had been ordered to reinforce the Northern Army in Canada, but as the regiment reached the St. Lawrence River, a smallpox epidemic, more deadly than any human enemy, overwhelmed the Americans.

The Northern Army had assembled the previous summer in a bold but doomed effort to invade and take Canada during the early months of the Revolutionary War. After capturing some border forts and Montréal, a series of calamities, including the death of the army's gallant leader, General Richard Montgomery, stalled the Americans outside the walls of Québec City. The invaders were able to cling to their precarious gains until the onset of spring allowed thousands of British regulars to arrive from the Mother County to relieve the besieged city, pushing the Americans into hasty retreat west and then south to the Crown Point narrows on Lake Champlain.

With the first wave of sick and dying men, Beebe returned to the American headquarters at Crown

"The Death of General Montgomery in the Attack of Quebec, December 1775," by John Trumbull, presents an idealized image of an invasion that was a disaster.
Yale University Art Gallery

Point. The suffering continued on both sides of the lake. "Death is now become a daily visitant in the Camps. But as Little regarded as the singing of birds," he wrote. By his estimate four to five hundred men were "in the height of the smallpox."

The Hudson River, Lake George, Lake Champlain, and the Richelieu River formed a waterway from New York City to St. Jean in Canada, not far from Montréal. Except for a few portages, a traveler or an army could cover nearly the entire 300-plus miles by water. An express messenger might take a week to make the journey if conditions were favorable. In an era when reliable roads were nearly nonexistent, the Hudson/Champlain corridor was of vital strategic importance.

The Crown Point-Chimney Point narrows had been the site of French fortifications since 1731. After the French abandoned Lake Champlain in 1759 during

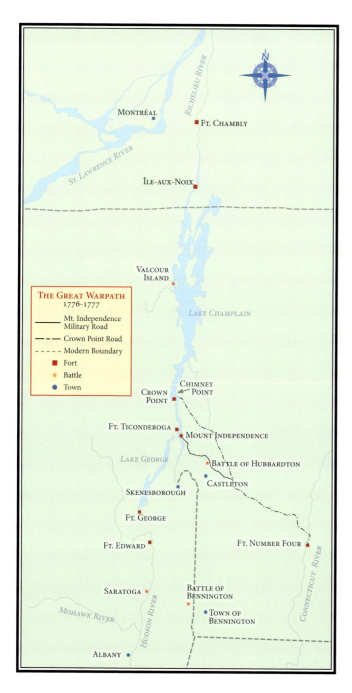

the French and Indian War (1754-1763), the British built Fort Crown Point, featuring 40-foot-high walls and a six-acre parade ground. The fort was destroyed by fire in 1773 and became, in the words of British military engineer John Montresor, "an amazing useless mass of Earth only." To rebuild would be a major undertaking, but most of the American army officers assumed that a stand would be made at Crown Point against a certain British attack from Canada.

On the rainy evening of July 5, 1776, three generals—Philip Schuyler, Horatio Gates, and Benedict Arnold—arrived at Crown Point from the south.

Brigadier General Arnold, 35 years old from New Haven, Connecticut, had emerged from the defeat in Canada as a hero. He led a thousand men through the Maine wilderness to Québec and maintained the siege through the winter after the death of commander

Map at left: Lake Champlain was part of a waterway broken by portages that stretched from New York to Canada and Montréal. Ticonderoga and Mount Independence were located at the important portage from Lake George. Steve Zeoli map

Small map: The narrows at Crown Point and Chimney Point as shown on a 1778-1779 British map. Library of Congress

Photo below: Crown Point was the largest British fort built during the French and Indian War. Burned in 1773, the remains of the stone barracks within the earthen walls can still be visited at the state historic site in Crown Point, New York. Courtesy Crown Point State Historic Site

SCHUYLER'S DECISION 7

As a young staff officer, John Trumbull, who first explored Mount Independence, drew this map of the fortifications and encampments as they existed in the summer of 1776.
Charles Allen Munn Collection, Fordham University Library, Bronx, N.Y.

Richard Montgomery. People were comparing Arnold to Hannibal, the ancient Carthaginian general who had crossed the Alps to attack Rome.

Major General Gates, nearly 49, had been a career British officer until he could rise no further in rank. In 1772, he settled in Virginia (today's West Virginia). He was George Washington's adjutant general outside Boston before the Continental Congress appointed him to an independent command in Canada. Gates was eager to take charge in the North, but there was no longer an army in Canada.

In June 1775, Schuyler had been appointed major

John Trumbull, self-portrait, 1777 Museum of Fine Arts – Boston

general and commander of the Northern Department, which included Lake Champlain. Although he had been in Canada only briefly, he had directed the invasion from Albany. He was a senior officer to Gates and maintained that the army at Crown Point was part of his command.

The two generals eventually agreed to cooperate, reaching an accommodation that satisfied neither man: Schuyler would command on paper from Albany, but Gates would exercise direct control of the army on Lake Champlain.

The newly arrived generals were appalled by what they saw at Crown Point. Schuyler reported to Washington, "The most descriptive pen cannot describe the Condition of our Army: Sickness, Disorder, and Discord, reign triumphant—the latter occasioned by an illiberal and destructive Jealousy, which unhappily subsists between the Troops raised in the different Colonies."

Since early June, Schuyler had been considering fortifying a rugged peninsula opposite Fort Ticonderoga, 13 miles south of Crown Point, at another narrows on the lake. Everyone had heard of Ticonderoga from the French and Indian War, but Schuyler's new site, soon to be named Mount Independence, was almost unknown. In the French and Indian War, French soldiers cut wood and quarried stone there, but their fort was on the west side of the lake. Called Carillon by its French builders, it gained its reputation in 1758 when soldiers under the Marquis de Montcalm defeated the largest British and Provincial

An Aristocratic General Surrounded by Controversy

Philip Schuyler (1733-1804), who made the decision to fortify Mount Independence, was a congressman in June 1775 when he was chosen by the Continental Congress as a major general and the commander in New York. Schuyler owned a mansion in Albany, river sloops on the Hudson, and mills and vast landholdings in Saratoga, today's Schuylerville. He had business and family ties to even wealthier aristocrats, the Livingstons, Van Cortlandts, and Van Rensselaers.

In the French and Indian War, Schuyler served as deputy commissary officer and had little opportunity to command men in the field, but he mastered the business of supplying an army. At the start of the Revolutionary War, he was ordered to invade Canada by way of Lake Champlain. Too sick to command in person, Schuyler oversaw the efforts to make Canada the 14th colony from his headquarters in Albany.

Schuyler spent only a few days at the Lake Champlain forts during 1776 and 1777. Other officers—notably Horatio Gates, Anthony Wayne, and Arthur St. Clair—commanded at the lake and reported to him, sometimes finding the relationship frustrating.

With men and women of wealth and position, Schuyler was gracious and generous. However, he squabbled with other officers and with the Continental Congress, often over petty issues. He had little respect for New Englanders or for common soldiers. At times, rumors circulated that he was a coward or even a traitor. In fact, he was fussy and painstaking, and the American cause benefitted from his diligence.

Philip Schuyler by John Trumbull, 1792.
Yale University Art Gallery

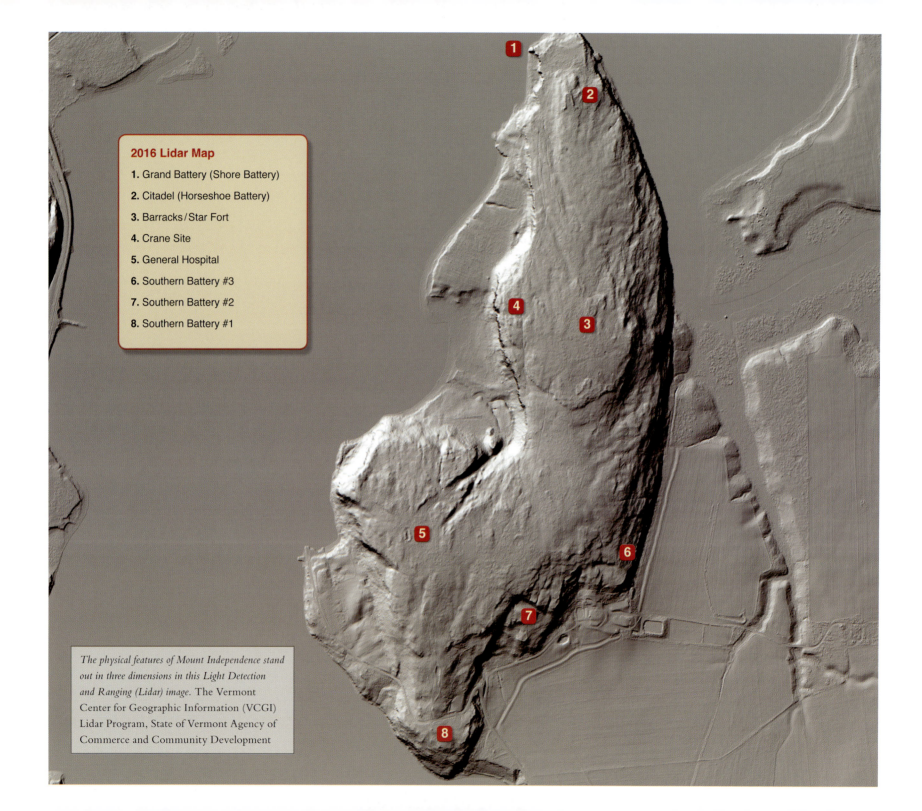

2016 Lidar Map

1. Grand Battery (Shore Battery)
2. Citadel (Horseshoe Battery)
3. Barracks/Star Fort
4. Crane Site
5. General Hospital
6. Southern Battery #3
7. Southern Battery #2
8. Southern Battery #1

The physical features of Mount Independence stand out in three dimensions in this Light Detection and Ranging (Lidar) image. The Vermont Center for Geographic Information (VCGI) Lidar Program, State of Vermont Agency of Commerce and Community Development

army yet assembled in North America. After the British under Sir Jeffrey Amherst captured the fort a year later, they rebuilt it, naming it Fort Ticonderoga, but soon mighty Crown Point became their focus.

On May 10, 1775, three weeks after the start of the Revolutionary War, Ethan Allen and Benedict Arnold gave the American colonies their first offensive victory by surprising Fort Ticonderoga's sleeping garrison of 44 British soldiers and 24 women and children.

However, the old fort was at the southern end of Ticonderoga peninsula, where it could not defend against an attack from the north, and it was in serious disrepair. Logs were rotting, and stonework was collapsing. In the summer of 1775, Schuyler had made his headquarters in the stone barracks of the old fort and was familiar with its weaknesses: "In my opinion a post on the Ground opposite to it would more effectively secure us against the Enemy."

On their way to take command of the army at Crown Point, Schuyler and Gates left 20-year-old Colonel John Trumbull to evaluate the site across the lake from Ticonderoga in what would later become Vermont. A promising artist, Trumbull was Gates's adjutant and the son of the governor of Connecticut. Today his dramatic paintings of pivotal events in the Revolution hang in the U.S. Capitol Rotunda and major museums.

For most of an afternoon, Trumbull, in company with New York Colonel Cornelius Wynkoop, explored the mile-and-a-quarter-long peninsula and the creek that entered Lake Champlain to the east. The land was

In Their Own Words:

After five days work on Mount Independence, engineer Jeduthan Baldwin nearly resigned his commission. At the time he was sleeping on the Ticonderoga side of the lake and crossing to East Point each morning. This account, complete with his distinctive spelling and lack of punctuation, comes from his journal.

July 16, 1776

In the morning between day and sunrise I heard some persons say that how come that Chest open, another person answered somebody had robd it they have pulld up the tent pins & taken the chest out, upon which I arose in my shirt & went out & found 2 friendly Officers lamenting my loss, I examined & found that I was robd of my Hatt, a Camblet Cloak a Surtoot, a blieu Coat & Jacoat trimed with a narrow Gold lace, a pair of Silk breeches, a Snuff coloured Coat turned up with white, a Velvet Jacoat, 3 Cotton & 3 Wollon Shirts, 3 Stocks, 2 linen Handkfs, 2 pair of linen & 2 pair of woolen Stockings, a pair of Silver Shoe & knee buckels, a Surveyors Compass or theodiler, & between 35 & 40 Dollars in paper money, an ink pot, n knife, key & a Number of papers & other articles.

I immediately sent to all the Commanding officers present, & at the landing, acquainting them with my loss, the Army was all turned out & a genl. Sirch made but none of my things found. I borrowed of a friend, a Coat & Jacoat & hatt, for I had none lift, I was Stript to my Shirt, my breeches & watch that lay under my head were saved only. Just at evening I heard that my coat turned up with white & Velvet Jacoat was found with the buckles &c. in the pockets, hid in a blind place.

July 17, 1776

In the Morning a part of my Compass was found broak to pieces & soon after the rest of it except the Needle. This Day I wrote to Genl. Sullivan to remind him of the request I had made of a discharge from the Army, desiring him to use his intrest in my behalf while at the Congress, as I am heartily tired of this Retreating, Raged Starved, lousey, thievish, Pockey Army in this unhealthy Country.

Mount Independence as seen from Mount Defiance on the New York side of Lake Champlain. The Ticonderoga peninsula is on the left. Vermont's Green Mountains are in the distance.
Guyland Ziebert photo

covered with "primeval forest," Trumbull recalled in his memoir, but the two colonels concluded it "was finely adapted for a military post." On three sides, the peninsula was surrounded by "a natural wall of rock, everywhere steep, and sometimes an absolute precipice sinking to the lake." The fourth side was creek and marsh, leaving only a narrow corridor at the southeastern end for a road to descend to the lake and into the countryside.

On July 7 at Crown Point, Schuyler presided over a council of war, which included Gates and Arnold as well as Brigadier General John Sullivan of New Hampshire, and Frederick William, Baron de Woedtke, a brigadier from the German kingdom of Prussia.

The council first resolved to leave Crown Point, which they judged to be indefensible by their present army. They ordered the sick to Fort George at the southern end of Lake George. They decided "to secure our superiority on Lake Champlain" by constructing a fleet of "gondolas, row-galleys, armed batteaus, &c." Finally, adopting Schuyler's viewpoint, they resolved that the army should "retire immediately to the strong ground, on the east side of the Lake opposite to Ticonderoga."

The decision shocked many officers, especially New Englanders. In response, 21 field officers led by Colonel John Stark of New Hampshire, formerly a captain in Roger's Rangers in the French and Indian War, signed a "remonstrance" objecting to the move. "We cannot but judge from our own observation of the ground here [Crown Point], that we can maintain it against any forces our enemy can send against us," they wrote Schuyler. Crown Point protected New England, they believed, and was the only location "where we can maintain a naval superiority upon the lakes."

Schuyler was angered and embarrassed at being challenged, but was adamant. The move was "not only prudent, but indispensably necessary," he responded tersely. After returning to his home and headquarters in Albany, he wrote to General Washington that the site of the new encampment and fortification is "so remarkably strong as to require little Labour to make it tenable against a vast superiority of Force, and fully to answer the purpose of preventing the Enemy from penetrating into the Country to the South of it."

Schuyler's letter and the objections of the field officers reached Washington's headquarters at the tip of Manhattan on the evening of July 16, 1776. Wash-

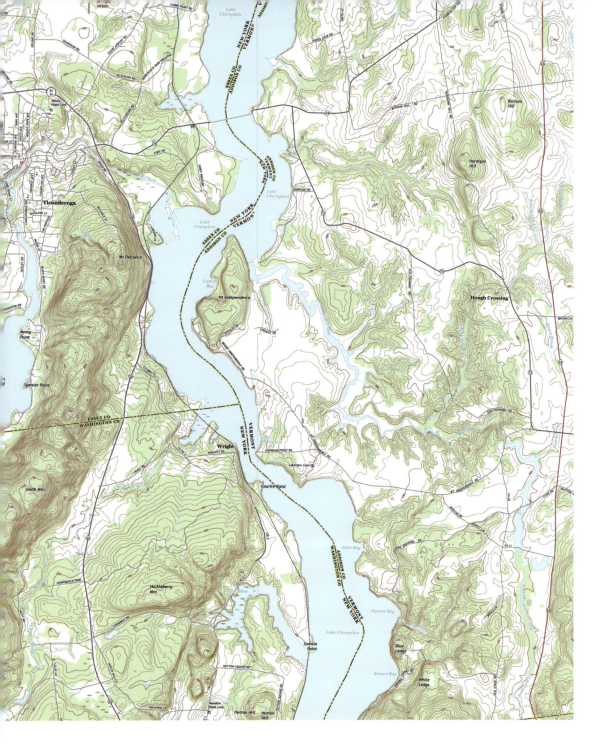

ington later told Gates, "Upon the whole, no event that I have been informed of for a long time produced a more general Chagrin and Consternation." Washington did not approve of officers contradicting their superiors, but told Schuyler, "The reasons assigned by the officers in their Remonstrance, appear to me forcible & of great Weight. They coincide with my own ideas." However, he did not order the army to remain at Crown Point, understanding that by the time letters made it back and forth, the move would be underway. Still, he told Gates that he wished "the measure could yet be changed with propriety."

Stung by Washington's criticism, Schuyler sent a lengthy justification of his decision. An army at Crown Point could be cut off by land and water, he argued. The combination of Ticonderoga and the new fortifications on the east side had none of the weaknesses of Crown Point. The supply routes across Lake George and from Skenesborough (today's Whitehall, New York) were protected. If Ticonderoga fell, the army would be secure in its new fortifications, but could retreat southward to Fort Edward on the Hudson River, if necessary. "Can they drive us out of the strong camp on the east side? I think not. I think it impossible for twenty thousand men to do it, ever so well provided, if the camp consists of less than even a quarter of that number, indifferently furnished, such is the natural strength of the ground."

2015-2016 topographical map of the Mount Independence/Ticonderoga area. USGS US Topo

Before Written History

An 18th century watercolor shows an Abenaki couple—City of Montréal Archives

Archaeologists have found evidence of people along the Lake Champlain shore near Mount Independence beginning in the Late Archaic Period, 6,000 years ago. More than 50 prehistoric sites have been discovered near Mount Independence on the shore of the lake or along East Creek. The wetlands of this slow-moving stream were a rich source of fish, freshwater mussels, ducks and geese, beaver, deer, and other animals.

High-quality blue-black chert, a hard, fine-grained sedimentary rock, can be found on Mount Independence. This chert is ideal for carving into tools and projectile points and was prized by the early people in the Champlain Valley. Traded widely, Mount Independence chert has been found by archaeologists at sites in New Hampshire and Maine.

By the time of European contact, the people inhabiting Vermont were Abenaki, the People of the Dawn, known to themselves as *Alnôbak* or "Real People." Lake Champlain was "Lake Between" or *Bitawbagok*, the boundary between them and the Iroquoian people.

Samuel de Champlain was the first European to visit the lake that bears his name. On July 30, 1609, he fought alongside his Native American allies against the Iroquois in a battle that took place on the west side of the lake either on the Ticonderoga peninsula, opposite Mount Independence, or at Crown Point.

"I have my hands & mind constantly employed night & Day except when I am a Sleep & then sometimes I dream."

— Jeduthan Baldwin, July 28, 1776

16 Strong Ground

CHAPTER TWO

Under the Direction of Jeduthan Baldwin

Development of the American defenses was put in the hands of a 44-year-old veteran of the French and Indian War from North Brookfield, Massachusetts. Lieutenant Colonel Jeduthan Baldwin first set foot on the peninsula opposite Ticonderoga on July 8, 1776, walking the ground with John Trumbull. He was back the next day, making plans with generals Schuyler and Gates. The following day, he, Trumbull, and Colonel Anthony Wayne of Pennsylvania marked a road from the lake to the top of the hill.

Baldwin was the Northern Army's authority on fortifications, although he lacked the formal training of European professionals. Military engineering was art, science, and mathematics, all conducted in elegant French. Largely self-taught, Baldwin brought to his assignment Yankee ingenuity and perseverance. The journal he kept during the early years of the Revolutionary War is an indispensable source of information about the development of Mount Independence.

The work of turning the rugged peninsula into a fortification began on July 11, when a 200-man party of Pennsylvanians under Baldwin's direction crossed Lake Champlain in bateaux during a rainstorm and started clearing the road and excavating a well. Baldwin and his work crews were so busy over the next few days that he simply recorded in his journal, "on the East point as Usual."

Though the peninsula was a "howling Wilderness," in the words of Ensign Bayze Wells of Charles Burrall's Connecticut State Regiment, the work of turning the ground into an organized camp progressed quickly. John Greenwood of John Paterson's 15th Continental Infantry from Massachusetts was a 16-year-old fifer at the time. The promontory was "thick with woods," he recalled years later, "and, being also very rocky, was filled with snakes of every description, though mostly black and rattlesnakes. Had it been filled with devils, however, it would have made no difference to our soldiers, for they were proof against everything."

In this drawing on the opposite page, noted historian and artist Gary Zaboly depicts life on Mount Independence in the summer of 1776. The man lying on the ground is Zephaniah Shepardson of Bedel's New Hampshire Rangers. As Shepardson told the story, after a few days under a doctor's care, he returned to his hut to find that his messmates had accepted another man in his place. He lay outside on pieces of bark with a low, crude roof to cover him. He wrote, "My simple, sickly baby thoughts were this: I thought I had no friends nor foes untill my hon[ored] father came unexpected to my relief." The elder Shepardson found a substitute soldier, mounted his son on a horse, and took him home. In the scene men play an early ball and bat game called wicket Gary Zaboly / Mount Independence Coalition

An early British map showing General Abercrombie's disastrous attack of the French Lines outside Fort Carillon in 1758. These fortifications were rebuilt during the Revolution by the Pennsylvania battalions but were still referred to as the French Lines.
Toronto Public Library.

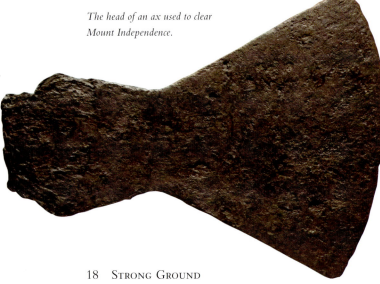

The head of an ax used to clear Mount Independence.

Naturally, some referred to the point as Rattlesnake Hill.

As the work progressed, the men began to occupy the point. A map drawn by Trumbull shows the location of the brigades and the layout of the camps, which followed Humphrey Bland's *Treatise of Military Discipline*, a British handbook studied closely by American officers. Bland set out precise scale drawings, measured in paces, illustrating the design of a camp, the guard, the parade ground, the placement of the colors, the tents of the rank and file, the tents of the officers in ascending rank, and the location of the privies.

Nine regiments from New England, two from New Jersey, and one from New York were divided into three brigades and ordered to clear "East Point" for camps and fortifications. Benedict Arnold commanded the First Brigade, to be quartered on the high flat ground above the northern point. In August, when he took command of the Lake Champlain fleet, Colonel John Greaton of Massachusetts acted as First Brigade commander. Colonel James Reed of New Hampshire and then Colonel John Paterson of Massachusetts commanded the Second Brigade, located on the southwestern part of the peninsula. John Stark commanded the centrally located Third Brigade. Briefly his men insisted that the peninsula be called "Stark's Point."

A cultural divide separated the Pennsylvania troops, encamped on the Ticonderoga side, from the New Englanders on the east side of the lake. Captain Persifor Frazer of Wayne's Fourth Pennsylvania Battalion wrote his wife, "The miserable appearance and what is worse the miserable behaviour of the Yankees is sufficient to make one sick of the service, they are by no means fit to endure hardships, among them there is the strangest mixture of Negroes, Indians and Whites with Old Men and mere children which together with a Nasty lousy appearance, makes a most shocking Spectacle." This animosity is one of the reasons Gates kept the lake between the Pennsylvanians and the New Englanders.

Zephaniah Shepardson of Timothy Bedel's New Hampshire Rangers helped construct a hut of logs with split logs for flooring and a roof of basswood bark. Some huts like Shepardson's had stone chimneys, others stick and daub, and still others a simple hole in the roof. Archaeological evidence suggests that officers lived in frame houses requiring nails, while enlisted men built log dwellings. No window glass has been found.

Word that Congress had declared independence from Great Britain reached the posts on July 15. On July 28, Colonel Arthur St. Clair read the document to the troops. St. Clair, commander of the Fourth Brigade, was a former British officer with an

Colonel John Stark, commander of the 5th Continental Infantry (New Hampshire) and the Third Brigade. As found in Centennial Anniversary of the Independence of the State of Vermont and the Battle of Bennington, August 15 and 16, 1877 (1879)

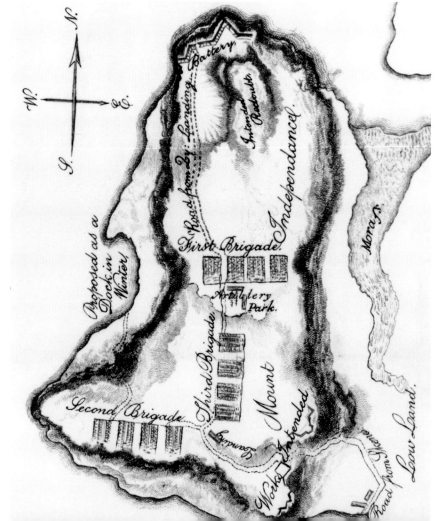

In a version of a map first drawn in 1776, John Trumbull depicted the camps on Mount Independence, which were constructed according to the standards laid out in a British handbook on military discipline. Autobiography, Reminiscences and Letters of John Trumbull, from 1756 to 1841

A uniform button of the Fifth Continental Infantry or John Stark's Regiment found by archaeologists at Mount Independence.

A medicine vial found by archaeologists on Mount Independence. It likely contained an opiate.

Right: Artist Greg Harlin captured the horror of hospitals at Mount Independence in a 1998 illustration for Smithsonian *magazine.*
Collection of the Mount Independence State Historic Site

impressive military bearing and the education to do justice to soaring rhetoric. "*God* save the free independent States of *America*!" St. Clair called out at the end, and the soldiers responded with three cheers. An observer, whose name is lost to history, reported, "It was remarkably pleasing to see the spirits of the soldiers so raised, after all their calamities; the language of every man's countenance was, Now we are a people; we have a name among the States of this world." From that day forward, East Point or Rattlesnake Hill took on its lasting name: Mount Independence.

The summer was wet. After a torrential downpour on the night of July 18–19, Dr. Lewis Beebe wrote, "Many of the sick Lay their whole lengths in water, with one blanket only to Cover them." He reported the sad fate of one sick soldier who drowned in his tent.

While smallpox was largely under control, other illnesses swept through the ranks. Standing water was a breeding ground for mosquitoes, leading to intermittent fevers such as malaria. Poor sanitation resulted in dysentery. With no scientific understanding of how disease spread, men blamed the air of Mount Independence. Trumbull recalled in his 1841 memoir, "The exhalations from the earth, which was now, for the first time, exposed to the rays of a midsummer sun, combined with the fog which rose from the pestilent lake, soon produced sickness in a new shape—a fever very nearly resembling the yellow fever of the pres-

Diversity in the Ranks

The American army on Mount Independence was multiracial, a fact that shocked officers of the Pennsylvania regiments at Ticonderoga. It is impossible to know how many blacks served on Mount Independence, but an estimated 5,000 fought for the cause of American liberty. Far more African Americans joined the British army, especially in the South where slavery was more prevalent, as they weighed which side would offer greater freedom. A few served in German regiments. When one battalion from the principality of Braunschweig (Brunswick in English) came home, they marched to the beat of African-American drummers.

The Native Americans at the Lake Champlain forts were Mohicans from Stockbridge, Massachusetts. They were ordered to wear blue and red caps to distinguish them from the Indians with the British army, so that "we may not by mistake kill our friends instead of our enemies." They were used as scouts, and some fought at the Battle of Valcour Island.

Black soldiers were often given menial work as servants or laborers, but they also served heroically at the battles of Valcour Island and Hubbardton.

As harsh as it was, military life offered African Americans opportunities to improve their situation. Jacob Down escaped slavery in Pennsylvania and joined a Massachusetts regiment stationed on Mount Independence. By chance, he was seen by his former owner, Captain Persifor Frazer, who demanded his property. Down's captain intervened and paid for his freedom.

Left: Agrippa Hull. The Stockbridge Library, Museum & Archives. *Right: A Stockbridge Indian as drawn in 1778 by a German soldier in New York.* Johann von Ewald / Harvey A. Andruss Library, Bloomsburg University of Pennsylvania

At least two blacks who spent time at Mount Independence, Agrippa Hull (1759-1848) and Lemuel Haynes (1753-1833), gained wider recognition, although both suffered from racism.

Hull was 18 years old and Brigadier General John Paterson's servant in the spring of 1777 when he met Polish military engineer Thaddeus Kosciuszko. During the brutal Southern Campaigns at the end of the war, he was Kosciuszko's orderly. He lived a long life in Stockbridge, Massachusetts, where, although poor, he received recognition as a notable person. His daguerreotype was taken in 1844, and today his portrait hangs in the town library.

Haynes was part of the militia that marched north to the Lake Champlain forts in the fall of 1776. Although his father was said to be of "unmingled African extraction," he became a respected pastor to white congregations in western Vermont and Washington County, New York. In 1801, on the 25th anniversary of American independence, the Reverend Haynes gave the address in Rutland. He said his listeners could search the entire world and not find a more free, secure, and happy country than America. "Still it is a land of improvement; we are not to conclude that the fair tree of liberty hath reached its highest zenith; may we not add to its lustre."

ent time—and it was not unusual to see the strongest men carried off by it in two or three days." Physicians recommended that large fires be lit on Mount Independence to purify the air.

The General Return for August 24, which showed more than 5,000 men in the Mount Independence brigades, tallied 1,005 rank-and-file soldiers as sick but present. Another 628 were sick but absent. In some regiments more than half the men were ill. Hundreds of men were "on command," meaning they were serving elsewhere, many with the Lake Champlain fleet. On September 8, Chaplain Ammi Robbins visited "tent by tent and could not pass one single tent among the soldiers wherein there were not one or more sick."

The officer corps was hard hit as well. Colonel William Bond, commander of the 25th Continental Regiment died of what was called bilious, putrid, or yellow fever. Colonel Greaton was sent to the hospital at Fort George at the southern end of nearby Lake George. Colonel Reed, the original commander of the Second Brigade, went blind from smallpox. Lieutenant Colonel Joseph Wait, in command of Bedel's Rangers, died at the end of September. Both colonels Burrall and Elisha Porter were sick. "There is something more than ordinarily solemn and touching in our funerals, especially an officer's," wrote Robbins. "Swords and arms inverted, others with their arms folded across their breast stepping slowly to the beat of the muffled drum."

With a combination of inspiration and disapproval, Gates attempted to get the most from men who were sick or under constant threat of disease and death. He

This magnificent powder horn belonged to John Calfe of Hampstead, New Hampshire, who served on Mount Independence in the spring of 1777. At the right, it shows the major fortifications: the Grand Battery, the Citadel, and the Star Fort; the Ticonderoga fortifications are depicted on the left." New Hampshire Historical Society

expressed shock at "the shameful dilatoriness with which the publick works are carried on Mount Independence," but encouraged the troops in his General Orders, "The same heats and colds that affect us affect our enemies...and shall *Americans*, whose all is at stake, want that firmness to animate them to arms which is necessary to defeat the unprincipled mercenaries of an unrelenting tyrant?"

Despite the prevalence of sickness in the camp, work to improve the fortifications continued. In his journal, Baldwin listed the craftsmen under his command: house and ship carpenters; blacksmiths; armorers, who repaired weapons; rope, wheel, and carriage makers; miners, who used gunpowder to blast rocks; turners, who operated lathes; colliers, who made the charcoal that was necessary for the forges; sawyers; and shingle makers. He also directed the fatigue parties, the laborers who cut and hauled wood, moved rock and earth. In the long daylight hours of summer, fatigue parties began work at 6 a.m., took an hour at noon for dinner, and then worked until 7 p.m. Baldwin commented, "I have my hands & mind constantly employed night & Day except when I am a Sleep & then sometimes I dream."

At the northern point, Baldwin laid out an artillery battery close to the lake with breastworks of stone and interlocked bundles of branches, known as fascines, all of which were covered with sod. A tangle of sharpened branches called abatis added protection against enemy

By the fall of 1776, the high ground of the Citadel was armed with five guns. The view looks across the quarter-mile-wide narrows of Lake Champlain toward reconstructed Fort Ticonderoga.

Left: Today a clearing marks the site of the Star Fort, which enclosed four acres and eight barracks. The view looks north toward Lake Champlain and the Ticonderoga peninsula. Alan Nyiri photo

Right: The foundation of an officer's house in the Third Brigade.

troops attempting to storm the breastworks. A few cannon were mounted by August 11. By the late fall, the Grand Battery was armed with 28 guns, including a massive 32-pounder, two 18s, and three 12s. Guns were defined by the weight of iron shot they could hurl. This ship-splintering concentration of firepower was the largest on either side of the lake.

Baldwin laid out another work on the rocky heights above the Grand Battery. Built of earth and shaped like a horseshoe, the Citadel could dominate the west side of the lake if the British took control of the Ticonderoga peninsula. By fall it was armed with five cannon.

Along the eastern rim of Mount Independence for more than a mile, men built breastworks of stone and logs, fronted by abatis. Across the top of the Mount, they constructed guardhouses, a bake house, a munitions laboratory, shops for artificers (skilled craftsmen), storehouses, and hospitals.

Early in September, Baldwin fell seriously ill. He tried various self-prescribed cures and continued to work. The herb camphor made him sweat all night, and in the morning he took rhubarb as a laxative, which "workt very kindly." On September 8, he laid out additional fortifications on the Ticonderoga side that came to be called Mount Hope. On September 10, he admitted he was too sick to work: "pain in my head across my Eyes & in my Stomach & Sick at the Stomach but could get nothing to take & so woried the Day thro." Then he was he hit with the ague, a fierce intermittent fever. By September 16, he felt a little better and thanked the Lord that he was alive. Still, he had to endure a rash that "burnt & is Very tedious to bair."

The chief engineer's health had improved by the end of September. He toured Mount Independence in company with Gates, St. Clair, and Trumbull to view the location for a fort on the highest ground. For several days he drew plans, and then began to stake out the walls with the help of new assistant engineer Christophe Pélissier, who was born in France and had directed the Saint-Maurice Ironworks at Trois-Rivières in Canada. Perhaps Pélissier questioned Baldwin's design, for the next day Baldwin, Pélissier, and others laid out the fort "agreeable to a New Plan I had drawn."

In the shape of an eight-pointed star, the walls were to be upright logs, or pickets, enclosing more than four acres and eight barracks. Star-shaped fortifications, which allowed for interlocking fields of fire, were the pinnacle of military engineering. Although the charred remains of Baldwin's fort rotted away long ago, images were preserved on exquisite powder horns engraved by men who labored there or occupied the fort the following the spring.

Meanwhile, the British and their German allies were massing on the Canadian border, preparing to sail south and "pay a visit." Gates was anxious that the "Publick Works" on Mount Independence be formidable. In the General Orders, Gates reminded his men, "A short time will determine whether we are to be freemen or slaves. Let us not loose the precious moment, but by perseverance & manly fortitude shew we are determin'd to conquer and be free."

The Triumphs and Defeats of a Popular General

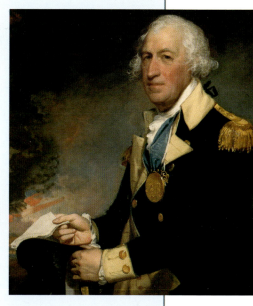

Major General Horatio Gates (1727–1806), commander at Ticonderoga and Mount Independence in the summer and fall of 1776, came from a humble, respectable background, although rumor had it that there was more to his story. His mother had been a housekeeper for the Duke of Leeds and then the Duke of Bolton. His father was a boatman on the Thames River who became a customs official after marriage and Horatio's birth. Perhaps the baby was actually the illegitimate son of someone of importance.

Unlike Philip Schuyler, his rival for command, Gates had the common touch and was popular with New Englanders and the militia. Although outwardly mild-mannered and a good companion, he could be ruthless in the political infighting that defined the Continental Army.

In 1777, he was the victor at Saratoga, often considered the turning point of the war because it led to an alliance with France. "Your Name Sir will be written in the breasts of the grateful Americans of the present Age & sent down to Posterity in Characters which will remain indelible when the Gold shall have changed its appearance," wrote Henry Laurens, president of the Continental Congress.

But posterity turned away. Gates played a murky role in efforts to replace George Washington as commander in chief, and his reputation suffered. Then at the Battle of Camden in South Carolina in August 1780, his force of thirty-seven hundred men was routed by General Cornwallis. Gates rode away from his defeated army. "One hundred and eighty miles in three days and a half. It does admirable credit to the activity of a man at his time of life," mocked Alexander Hamilton, who was soon to marry Schuyler's daughter Elizabeth.

Horatio Gates by Gilbert Stuart, c. 1794 Metropolitan Museum of Art

MASTERY OF LAKE CHAMPLAIN 25

CHAPTER THREE

Mastery of the Lake

"The near approach of the enemy, has as it were reanimated our officers, and put new life and vigor into our Soldiers. Every one exerts himself to the utmost, for an approaching battle—our works go on day and night without cessation." — DR. LEWIS BEEBE, OCTOBER 16, 1776

By the end of July 1776, Mount Independence and Ticonderoga stood at the heart of a web of forts, guard posts, hospitals, and depots, all part of the struggle to maintain control of Lake Champlain. Crown Point, 13 miles north, was still occupied by one regiment, the Sixth Pennsylvania Battalion. Thirty-five miles southwest of Ticonderoga, Fort George was the site of the largest hospital and was the point of departure for supplies and men to be shipped the length of Lake George for the army at the twin forts.

The July 7 council of war had resolved that "the most effectual Measures be taken to secure our Superiority on Lake Champlain by a naval armament of Gondaloes, Row Gallies, armed Batteaus, etc." Months before Philip Schuyler had established a shipyard in Skenesborough at the far south end of Lake Champlain. In the retreat from Canada, the army burned the shipyard at St. John (St. Jean) and seized every vessel on the upper Richelieu River, preventing the British from pursuing immediately. For the time being, the Americans held the advantage, but everyone knew it was a matter of time until the enemy had their own vessels on the lake. Building a navy became a race.

Impatient with the progress at the shipyard, General Gates blamed Schuyler for not arming the little fleet properly, for using the vessels as "Waggons" only, and for not building gondolas fast enough. "Sixty

After a day of fighting, October 11, 1776, the gondola Philadelphia, *manned by soldiers drafted from Mount Independence, sinks into Valcour Bay. Giving assistance is the battered row-galley* Washington, *which surrendered two days later. Today the* Philadelphia *can be seen at the Smithsonian National Museum of American History in Washington, D.C. The replica* Philadelphia II *is part of the Lake Champlain Maritime Museum in Ferrisburgh, Vermont.*
Ernest Haas /
Lake Champlain Maritime Museum

In 1942, as the United States strengthened its navy and merchant marine to fight World War II, illustrator Roy F. Heinrich imagined the building of the Lake Champlain fleet for a National Life of Vermont advertisement in The Saturday Evening Post *and* Life.
Roy F. Heinrich / Copyright National Life Group. Printed with permission

carpenters are now employed at Skenesborough," he complained to Schuyler on July 19. "They must be very ill-attended to, or very ignorant of their business, not to do more work. At this rate our superiority upon the Lake will be of short continuance." Finally, he sent Benedict Arnold to Skenesborough "to give life and spirit to our dock-yard."

As a man of action and the owner and captain of trading vessels out of Connecticut, Arnold was the natural choice to energize the effort to build the American navy on Lake Champlain. He found a thriving shipyard in Skenesborough, but one facing enormous supply and manpower problems. Nevertheless, four gondolas—unwieldy gunboats—were already built. Two more were in the stocks and would be finished in about a week, to be followed by a little sailing vessel that was variously called a gondola, galley, or cutter. More gunboats were in preparation, as was the first true row-galley, based on "the Spanish construction." A more maneuverable craft with lateen (triangular) sails and sweep oars, the row-galley was capable of mounting six or more heavy guns. When ship carpenters from Pennsylvania and Massachusetts arrived, Arnold ordered them to begin a second row-galley. "In two or three weeks, I think we shall have a very formidable fleet," he told Gates.

The hull and basic framework for these vessels were crafted in Skenesborough, then rowed north to Mount Independence and Fort Ticonderoga for the rigging that would make them warships, including the mounting of cannon. While there were plenty of guns to go around, carriages to mount them on were scarce. Colonel Baldwin reported in his journal on August 29 that, "we double mand our Smiths fires & workt in all the Shops both night & Day to get the Shiping riggd. & The artilery mounted."

At St. John, the British and German troops under Guy Carleton, governor-general of Québec, were constructing their own fleet. They began with craft to carry troops south in pursuit of the Americans even before the Northern Army had fully retreated from

Canada. But the Americans had a small navy on Lake Champlain, so the British army could not sail without exposing themselves to the three American armed schooners and one sloop.

The British had armed vessels on the St. Lawrence River, but 12 miles of rapids on the Richelieu River between Chambly and St. John blocked the way to Lake Champlain. They hoped to have oxen haul some vessels past the rapids on a new road, but instead the schooners *Maria* and *Carleton* were dismantled and reassembled at St. John. The gondola *Loyal Convert* was dragged through the rapids. These three vessels would be added to the fleet being built at St. John, which also included a massive barge-type craft called a radeau and named *Thunderer*, a floating fortress armed to the teeth with cannon.

Still not satisfied, Carleton ordered that a square-rigged ship under construction at Québec be transported to St. John and rebuilt. Eighty feet in length with 18 heavy guns, the *Inflexible* was by far the most powerful vessel of war on the lake.

When complete, the British fleet was impressive, but constructing it took time, which allowed the Americans to fortify Mount Independence, rebuild the French Lines—the fortification where Montcalm defeated General James Abercrombie in 1758—and restore an army that had been broken by defeat and disease. One anonymous correspondent writing from Mount Independence in the height of preparations expressed confidence in the American position. It may be Carleton's intention to "drive the rebels out of the country, and winter in Albany," he wrote on July 30, but first the British would have to pass the American navy, then Crown Point, and "thirdly, the narrows below Independent Point and Ticonderoga. Our fortifications are much stronger than when the French had this post, when, with only three thousand French and Canadians, they made such a terrible havock of the British army, in 1758." He then praised the "Good living" at the Mount, "having plenty of fresh beef and excellent bread."

Access to supplies and reinforcements was one of the main advantages of Mount Independence, along with its location on the Vermont shore. The water

Above: Events turned on the actions of Brigadier General Benedict Arnold, commander of the First Brigade on Mount Independence and then of the fleet. He was always controversial and frequently in conflict with other officers.
H.B. Hall after John Trumbull, U.S. National Archives

Left: Governor-General Sir Guy Carleton (1724-1808) was a cautious commander, who was criticized for not pressing his advantage in the fall of 1776. By the war's end, Carleton was commander-in-chief in North America. Today across Canada, there are institutions and place names honoring him. His statue as Baron Dorchester stands outside Parliament in Ottawa.
Library and Archives Canada

MASTERY OF LAKE CHAMPLAIN 29

What they ate and drank

The Continental Congress set what the ration should be for an enlisted soldier in the Continental Army. Each man was promised daily one pound of beef or three-quarters pound of pork, a pound of bread or flour, and a pint of milk. Every week soldiers were to receive three pints of peas, beans, or "vegetables equivalent." The ration might be supplemented with rice or cornmeal. For beverages, men were promised a quart of spruce beer or cider per day (or nine gallons of molasses to make rum, per company each week).

Early in the summer of 1776, troops at Mount Independence received three days of salt meat and four days of fresh each week. Later, as more cattle were herded to Lake George, butchered there, or taken live to the forts, men received fresh meat six days a week. Flour and salt meat were packed in barrels for transport. A barrel of meat and a barrel of flour supplied 200 men for a day—if the weight was honest, the flour was not spoiled by moisture, or the briny water preserving the meat drained to lighten a load.

A half-dozen soldiers cooked together as a group or mess, usually boiling their food in a cast iron pot or tin kettle. Women attached to the army as camp followers might do the cooking. Anthony Wayne ordered, "No Beef or other meats to be fry'd on any acct whatsoever." But archaeologists have found burned bones in many trash pits, along with "pot polished" boiled bones.

Fresh water was scarce on Mount Independence. Zephaniah Shepardson remembered, "There was but two springs on or under the hill which was three-quarters of a mile [from our hut]—small springs that would run into the nose of bottle or canteen—where 20 or 30 thirsty, dry soldiers was waiting for their turns for water all night."

Rum or other spirits were issued to men by the gill (four ounces) during inclement weather, especially in October 1776 when the forts expected to be attacked. Men could purchase liquor from the sutlers, who were strictly regulated in an unending battle against drunkenness.

In October, Horatio Gates wrote to Philip Schuyler about the sporadic supplies. Live cattle were "pretty plenty." Flour was scarcer than meat. "And where are the one or two thousand bushels of turnips and potatoes you was to send here?" In November, men complained that they could not work on a diet of meat only. When shipments of flour arrived, Anthony Wayne told the Pennsylvania Council of Safety that the men lacked "every necessary except flour and bad beef." A few days earlier, he had condemned almost 3,000 pounds of "fresh" meat, ordering it buried or burned.

The army moved on to Mount Independence too late in the summer of 1776 to plant gardens, but on April 2, 1777, engineer Jeduthan Baldwin "laid out a large gardin at ye foot of the Mount." Deer, ducks, geese, passenger pigeons, and fish supplemented the diet, as did the first greens of spring.

Jim Ross photo   Mount Independence State Historic Site photo

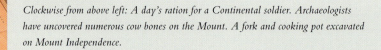

Clockwise from above left: A day's ration for a Continental soldier. Archaeologists have uncovered numerous cow bones on the Mount. A fork and cooking pot excavated on Mount Independence.

highway was one such route, but Schuyler's council of war in July had called for another, "a Road between the high Ground opposite to Ticonderoga" and "the Northern Settlements."

On September 7, Gates put this plan into action by ordering Lieutenant Colonel John Barrett of the New York militia to begin construction of the road from Rutland, in what would become Vermont, including the building of a "Good Bridge Over Otter Creek." When complete, this road would cut through the undulating terrain to the southeast of the Mount and connect in Rutland with the old Crown Point Road. It had been built during the French and Indian War to facilitate travel to Fort Number 4 along the Connecticut River in New Hampshire. The following day, Gates ordered that construction of the road begin from the southern base of the Mount. Once the two sections were joined and the new road was opened, troops and supplies could travel more easily from the central region of New England to Mount Independence.

With the building of a navy well underway, Horatio Gates turned command of the fleet over to Arnold, replacing Commodore Jacobus Wynkoop, who had been appointed by Schuyler. Gates told John Hancock, president of the Continental Congress, that Arnold was "perfectly skilled in maritime affairs." But the change in command was not smooth, and Arnold and Wynkoop clashed. On August 17, Wynkoop ordered his flagship, the *Royal Savage*, to fire a warning shot to stop two schooners that were acting under Arnold's orders. With Gates's agreement, Wynkoop was arrested and sent to Albany in disgrace.

On September 3, Gates reported to Washington, "The Fleet under General Arnold down the Lake is Increased to Twelve Sail Carrying Sixty Seven pieces

This flintlock musket was found in the lake along the shore of Mount Independence. It has been conserved and is now on display

1776 map of Lake Champlain. Library of Congress

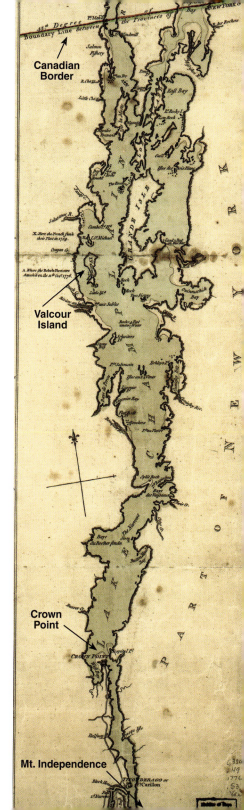

Both the exploding shell called a grenade (above) and the bar shot were found by underwater archaeologists off Mount Independence.

of Cannon, The Three Row Galleys, and one more Gondola, will be ready to Join The Fleet in ten or fifteen Days at farthest."

Arnold used his small flotilla to harass the British at the northern end of the lake, attempting to delay the enemy invasion from Canada as long as possible. But by early October Carleton was ready to sail. On October 11, his more powerful fleet encountered Arnold's fleet in the bay between Valcour Island and the New York shore south of the current city of Plattsburgh. By sunset, the American navy had sustained major damage, but remained intact. Arnold fled south under cover of darkness, and when the enemy threatened to overtake him on October 13, he ordered four gunboats and the galley *Congress* burned, before making his way back to the fortifications at Ticonderoga and Mount Independence.

The Battle of Valcour Island was a one-sided defeat for the American navy, but remains one of the most important military engagements of the war. The ragtag navy assembled by Schuyler, Gates, and Arnold forced Carleton to halt his rapid pursuit of the weakened Northern Army in order to build a navy of his own, giving the Americans a precious additional three months to recover their strength.

Throughout the summer of 1776, supplies were making their way northward to the twin fortifications, even if at a pace that left Gates frustrated. He continually wrote to Schuyler to request supplies and equipment. "I beg you will send me all the Spades you can collect as fast as possible," he demanded on October 15.

Nevertheless, preparations continued at Mount Independence and Fort Ticonderoga and conditions improved greatly. Surgeon Samuel Adams of Massachusetts recorded the transformation of the grounds and of the army in a letter home to his wife. "Mount Independence which 3 Months agone was a doleful Wilderness, & a haunt for wild beasts and Rattlesnakes," he wrote, "is now become a pleasant City, and we render our Soldier way of life less disagreeable then was at our first coming here. What we then thought hardships we [now] esteem but inconveniences."

Militia from all across the northeast poured into camp. Many of the sick began recovering health and rejoined their regiments. Three months of effort had turned the works at Ticonderoga and Mount Independence into a major defensive position. Arnold reflected the general optimism in a note to Schuyler. "The Season is so far advanced, our people are daily growing more healthy," he wrote on October 15. "We have about Nine thousand Effectives and if properly supported make no doubt of stopping the Career of the Enemy."

The British seized Crown Point, just 13 miles from the American defenses. Carleton sent parties to probe the American position on the west shore, one raid resulting in one dead American, two prisoners, and a herd of cattle. Gates sent out a squad to cut bridges and obstruct the road from Crown Point to prevent the British from hauling artillery by land.

The Americans waited for the British to attack. "We are expecting every Hour to be attacked by our Enemies," Jeduthan Baldwin wrote to his daughter Betsey. He promised to return home for the winter "if my life is spared." Gates issued orders directing how the regimental surgeons should be posted, ready to attend to the wounded. And Baldwin continued the urgent work of preparing the defenses. To prevent the British vessels from sailing down between the two peninsulas, Gates ordered the construction of a log boom to block the channel. Baldwin set his men to work and had this obstruction in place in eight days, and even added a floating bridge to facilitate the movement of troops between the two forts.

Between 11 p.m. and midnight on October 15, musket fire roused the entire garrison on Mount Independence for battle. But it was a false alarm. "Thro mistake the fire was at an ox, which was taken for the enemy, for not giving the Countersign when demanded," Dr. Lewis Beebe quipped in his journal.

Finally, on the morning of October 28, four British boats with heavy guns in their bows were seen off Three Mile Point. A guard boat gave the first alarm. At the Jersey Redoubt, a small fort by the lake on the

In Their Own Words:
BE YE NOT AFRAID OF THEM

Passages from a Sermon delivered on Mount Independence by Chaplain William Tenent, Sunday, October 20, 1776

The hour is expected, when, with the blessing of Heaven, you will have it in your power to do the most signal, important, and lasting service to your native land. She asks, she entreats, she calls, with a solemn, but pathetick tone, yea, she demands, your service, your most vigorous exertions, to save her from ruin….

When our enemy approaches, be ye not afraid of them; let not your spirits sink, but rather rejoice that you have an opportunity to contribute your whole might for the deliverance of your country from the disturbers of the common peace, and robbers of the rights of mankind….

Though transported from foreign climes, they are flesh and blood. They are but men, who are subject to the like hopes and fears with yourselves; and a ball well directed will humble them as quick as any, even the feeblest, of you. Be not ye, therefore, afraid of them, for they are not invincible.

Be not afraid of them, because they are engaged in a wicked and unrighteous cause, which the righteous Lord abhorreth. Be not afraid of them, though their numbers should be superiour to yours, because you are possessed of advantages which they have not: you have the ground and all the works you have made on it.

Be not afraid of them, because the want of courage will prove your ruin. There is nothing but victory or an honourable death before you. There is no retreat for you….

Your wives and children, your aged parents, your brethren and sisters, look to you, under God, for salvation. The peace of all our frontier inhabitants depends upon your success. You have the prayers of thousands for victory; and be assured, if you are victorious, the enemy will, from hence forward, cease to expect a submission from these United States. *If you are victorious, the virgins of our land and all your dear connexions will hail you welcome upon your return, with high applause and great joy; yea, Zion herself will be glad.*

The heavy guns on the Citadel (the Horseshoe Battery) and the Grand Battery are manned and await the British attack on October 28, 1776. Instead, seeing the strength of the American defenses, Governor-General Guy Carleton ordered his forces back to Canada for the winter.
Artwork by Gary Zaboly / Mount Independence Coalition

Ticonderoga side, men fired another signal shot. It was answered by a gun at the French Lines, a half mile northwest of old Fort Ticonderoga, and then by one on the Citadel on Mount Independence. Throughout the camps, drummers beat the call to arms. Believing the moment of truth had arrived, soldiers took their posts. Three regiments from Mount Independence—James Reed's 2nd Continental Infantry from New Hampshire, John Greaton's 24th Continental Infantry from Massachusetts, and Enoch Poor's 8th Continental Infantry from New Hampshire—were ferried across the narrows to reinforce the French Lines and the redoubts, the small forts built on the flat land close to the lake. Years later John Trumbull described the scene: "The whole summit of cleared land, on both sides of the lake, was crowned with redoubts and batteries, all manned with a splendid show of artillery and flags."

When one boat sailed closer, the Jersey Redoubt and the galleys *Trumbull* and *Gates* opened fire and drove it away. Americans believed that the "few merry shot from our Batteries" had been deadly. Men counted 17 boats in the distance and estimated that thousands of soldiers were coming ashore. An hour before sundown, they vanished.

In fact, this action by Carleton was merely another probe to reconnoiter the American defenses. What Carleton learned was that the American position was strong with gun batteries lining both sides of the lake and artillerymen who could shoot true. Baldwin's log boom blocked the lake. And as many as 14,000 soldiers manned the lines on the east and west shores, outnumbering his 8,000-man force. A long siege would last into the harsh winter. Already snow was falling and some of the bays were icing over.

As Carleton pondered the discouraging situation, the British returned to Crown Point and lingered there for a few more days. They set up advance posts several miles in front of their camps, which attracted Gates's attention. On the night of November 2 he ordered parties on both sides of the lake to attack these positions. When the two forces, led by Major James Dunlap and Lieutenant Colonel Samuel Connor, reached their targets at dawn, they discovered the sites abandoned. Not only were these outposts vacated, but scouting parties "found the enemy all gone" from Crown Point.

While no official words acknowledged it, the decision by Schuyler and the council of war to abandon Crown Point and to rely on the "strong ground" opposite Ticonderoga had been vindicated. Carleton's invasion had ground to a halt at the twin forts of Mount Independence and Ticonderoga. The British could not advance to Albany in 1776, giving the Americans a major victory at around the same time Washington's army was driven off Manhattan and into New Jersey. The British controlled the northern and southern ends of the strategic waterway between New York and Canada. The Americans held the upper Hudson River, Lake George, and the southern end of Lake Champlain, allowing them to maintain critical lines of communication between the New England states and those to the south. The fledgling United States had been preserved for another year.

A view from above the Citadel looking north. On October 28, 1776, the land was clear of trees, the defenses were manned by thousands of men, and British vessels approached from the north.
Alan Nyiri photo

The Battle of Valcour Island

"It is a defensive War we are carrying on," Horatio Gates told Benedict Arnold. "No wanton risque, or unnecessary Display of the Power of the Fleet, is at any Time, to influence your Conduct. Should the Enemy come up the Lake, and attempt to force their Way through the Pass you are stationed to defend in that Case you will act with cool determined Valour, as will give them Reason to repent their Temerity."

Gates believed the fleet should defend the narrows at Split Rock or at Île-aux-Têtes, near today's U.S.-Canadian border. Instead, Arnold chose to wait between Valcour Island and the western shore of the lake, about 60 miles from Mount Independence. He told Gates in a letter that his fleet was "moored ... as near together as possible. & in such a form that few Vessels can attack us at the same Time, & then will be exposed to the fire of the whole fleet." But he also claimed retreat was "open and Free," which it was not. Arnold's fleet of 15 vessels—two schooners, a sloop, three row-galleys, a cutter, and eight gunboats or gondolas—could be bottled up and destroyed.

The British fleet, which sailed south on October 11, outnumbered and outgunned the Americans, but as Arnold had recognized, they were at a disadvantage in the narrow bay with wind coming from the north. Still, in a daylong battle, the American schooner *Royal Savage* ran aground and was burned, and the gunboat *Philadelphia* sank. By the end of the day, other vessels were badly damaged and leaking, and the fleet had expended three-quarters of its ammunition.

In the dark, the 13 remaining vessels slipped between the British and the New York shore. Over a two-day pursuit, all but four were captured or destroyed. Arnold aboard the galley *Congress* escorted four gunboats into Ferris Bay (present-day Arnold Bay) and burned the vessels, flags flying, rather than to see them captured.

The Battle of Valcour Island is considered among the most heroic chapters in American military history. But what was accomplished? James Wilkinson, an unscrupulous but sometimes insightful staff officer at Ticonderoga, saw only "rashness and folly." Arnold's "naval adventure ... eventuated in heavy expenses, and the loss of many valuable lives, without a solitary ray of SOLID advantage to the public service," he wrote in his 1816 memoir.

But most famously, naval historian Alfred T. Mahan, a proponent of U.S. sea power, wrote in 1898, "The little American navy on Lake Champlain was wiped out, but never had any force, big or small, lived to better purpose or died more gloriously; for it had saved the lake for that year."

The Battle of Valcour Island 1776 by Henry Gilder Royal Collection Trust / © Her Majesty Queen Elizabeth II

36 STRONG GROUND

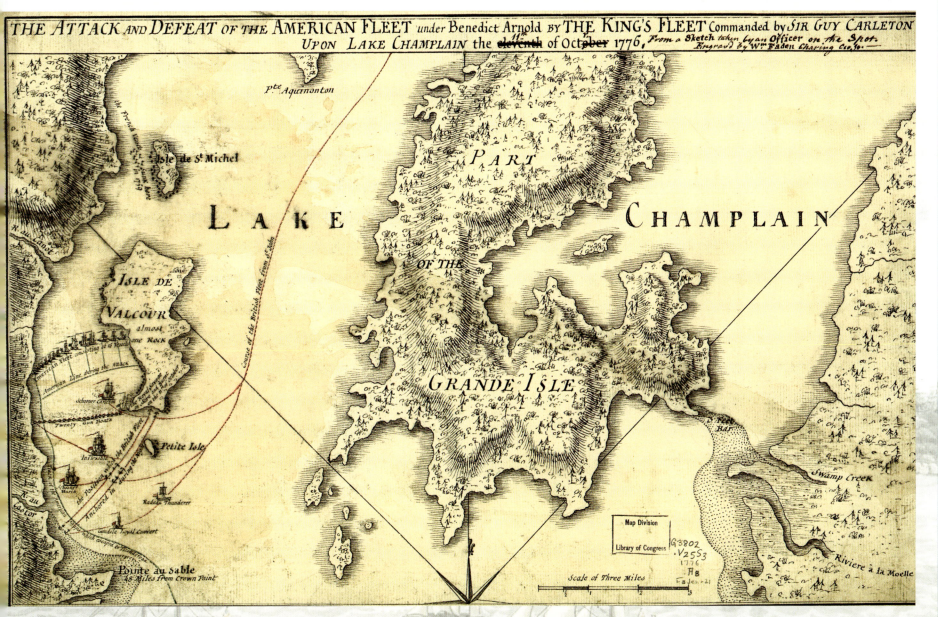

A British map engraved soon after the battle. Library of Congress

MASTERY OF LAKE CHAMPLAIN 37

38 Strong Ground

CHAPTER FOUR

A Long, Bitter Winter

"This day, though cold, the whole of the troops here were paraded on the ice, and continued going through sundry manuœvers for two or three hours, till we like to have perished." — LIEUTENANT EBENEZER ELMER, JANUARY 9, 1777

After the withdrawal of the British and their German auxiliaries to Canada, the American troops at Mount Independence and Ticonderoga began to stream south. General Gates and his staff tried to bring order to the exodus, but were not always successful. The tension of the fall had suddenly lifted, but winter was coming on fast, and provisions and firewood were scarce. A thousand militiamen who had rallied after the Battle of Valcour Island left first. Ten thousand men were still present for the November 9 General Return. In two weeks, the total of officers and men had dropped to fewer than 3,000.

"Wish we were not always betwixt hawk & Buzzard," commented Dr. Lewis Beebe while waiting to depart. "One day have orders to march for N. Hampshire; the next for Fort George, and the next for neither." Finally on November 16, Beebe, as part of a brigade of New England regiments, crossed the float bridge from Mount Independence, camped at Lake George Landing, and early the next morning embarked for Fort George.

On November 18, with a few regiments yet to march, generals Horatio Gates and Benedict Arnold departed Ticonderoga, leaving 31-year-old Colonel Anthony Wayne in charge. He was not yet known as "Mad Anthony," but already he had a reputation for bravery, a quick temper, and the highest standards. John Lacey, a captain in Wayne's Fourth Pennsylvania

During the winter of 1776-1777, frozen Lake Champlain was the parade ground for men at Ticonderoga and Mount Independence. On some days they drilled on the ice until they "almost perished" from the cold. In this scene, men from the Sixth Pennsylvania Battalion are drilling, 300 feet to the south of the Ticonderoga peninsula, with Fort Ticonderoga in the background.
Gary Zaboly /
Mount Independence Coalition

Anthony Wayne, commander of Mount Independence and Ticonderoga in the winter of 1776-1777.
Library of Congress

Facing page: The winter 1776-1777 encampment on Lake Champlain deserves to be remembered alongside Valley Forge and Morristown.
Greg Harlin for *Smithsonian* magazine/ Collection of Mount Independence State Historic Site

Battalion who would himself become a militia brigadier general, thought his colonel was a "Tyrant in his very Nature, of an implacable temper, once offended always cruel and unforgiving." But many others were inspired by this ambitious young commander, who had shown strong leadership in Canada during the defeat at Trois-Rivières in June. From Albany Gates wrote John Hancock, "He is a Capable good Officer, and has Health & Strength fit to Encounter the Inclemency of that Cold unhospitable Region."

Gates chose Wayne for the assignment—over the more senior colonels John Stark, Enoch Poor, and John Paterson—by ordering their regiments south to join George Washington. It was a mixed honor for Wayne. Young in years and seniority, he now had command of the major fortifications in the north and the responsibilities of a brigadier general. But Wayne did not like the region. In mid-December, he wrote to Congressman George Clymer of Pennsylvania that Ticonderoga "appears to be the last part of the world that God made. I have some ground to believe it was finished in the dark." He called it "the place of skulls," and provided gruesome details of how the men made use of the skeletal remains of soldiers killed during the French and Indian War, drinking from the skulls and hammering the leg bones into the ground as tent pegs.

Wayne's greatest frustration was not being able to join Washington in defense of Pennsylvania, his home state. In nearly every letter, he begged to be sent where the action was. On December 1, he told Congressman Richard Peters, "I have as yet 1500 hardy Veterans from Penn'a [Pennsylvania], would to Heaven I could for a day lead them to the Assistance of poor Washington." Wayne nevertheless remained the true soldier, promising Gates he would "render this place as tenable as possible."

Construction continued on Mount Independence well into November. Jeduthan Baldwin oversaw the building of post-and-beam barracks inside the picket fort. Men complained that it was difficult to work when their ration was only beef and no flour—just the start of the shortage of supplies that would plague the camp for several months.

Early in December, scouts returned from the north with news that a square-rigged vessel mounting 14 guns had anchored off Crown Point. Men at the forts were ordered to sleep with their muskets beside them that night, and in the morning they paraded to meet the expected attack. Finally, a bateau using blankets for sails arrived with a load of corn and potatoes from the Onion (Winooski) River. Relieved, the men enjoyed poking fun at the scouts for their mistake.

Winter was setting in early and hard. By December 11, thin ice covered Lake Champlain, except off the point of Mount Independence. Wind and waves had broken the float bridge and the boom, and moving between Mount Independence and Ticonderoga once again required boats until the lake froze over.

Ebenezer Elmer, a lieutenant with Colonel Elias Dayton's Third New Jersey Regiment, arrived at the Mount in early November. The young lieutenant suffered through illness during the latter part of the month and early December, but went about his duties. On December 2, he was a member of a party of 30 men who "went up to the mills for boards in flats." The day was cold and "the business tedious." It was dark by the time they were ready to shove off, and Elmer had to splash into the frigid water to help push the boats out from shore. By the time they landed back at the Mount around 8 o'clock, his soaked clothing had frozen.

When Wayne ordered the Third New Jersey to new quarters on Mount Independence, they had to break ice and fight a stiff wind as they rowed across the narrows. The men did not welcome the move to the new barracks in the picket fort. Just before sunset, Elmer and Ensign John Kinney carried their belongings up the hill to their new quarters. They gathered wood and lit a fire in a room with a dirt floor and no door. "The night was so excessively cold, and the room so open, I could not sleep," Elmer noted in his journal. "Indeed suffered most intolerably all night; learning some thing farther of the fatigues of a soldier's life."

Disease and cold stalked the camps on Lake Champlain. "It was never half so cold in Philada [Philadelphia] as this day," Colonel Joseph Wood, commander of St. Clair's old battalion, wrote financier Robert Morris in mid-December, "I had three men froze to Death last night, in there Tents. Colo Wayn four."

Despite the harshness of the northern winter, Wayne insisted on maintaining the strictest discipline. Guards posted to stand in the freezing weather were to be freshly shaved, their hair tied back and "well powdered." Occasionally, the discipline bordered on cruelty.

A LONG, BITTER WINTER 41

The Rusco Powder Horn

In the winter of 1776-1777, Sergeant David Rusco of Burrall's Connecticut State Regiment carved a powder horn that is one of the treasures on view at the Mount Independence Historic Site Visitor Center. Dated 1777, Rusco's powder horn depicts the fortifications on the Mount: the Star Fort and barracks, the Citadel, and the Grand Battery. Soldiers only had time to engrave these practical works of art when they were encamped for a long time.

Other men quartered on Mount Independence also carved powder horns during the winter and spring of 1777. Among the soldiers on the Mount must have been a gifted folk artist who could draw the lines to be engraved.

Rusco, who was born on Long Island in 1754, enlisted in Captain David Downs's Company of Burrall's Regiment on February 1, 1776. On May 19, he was captured by the British and their Indian allies at the Cedars, a stockade fort 30 miles west of Montréal. Benedict Arnold negotiated the release of the American prisoners, and Rusco joined the retreat from Canada to Lake Champlain. That summer Burrall's Regiment was part of the First Brigade on Mount Independence, commanded at the start by Arnold. After most regiments left the Lake Champlain forts in November, Burrall's men remained in the barracks on the Mount. The regiment was discharged in Albany on March 12, 1777.

In 1795, Rusco settled in Monkton, Vermont. He and his wife Silphina had six sons and five daughters. The couple died in 1832 within a few days of each other.

The powder horn was given to the Mount Independence Historic Site in 2003 in memory of George Roscoe (1915-1990).

On Christmas Day the entire garrison, "shav'd and powder'd," was ordered to parade and drill on the ice until two o'clock in the afternoon. The men "almost perished" from the cold, Elmer noted. On the following day, one man coming from Skenesborough died of exposure and his companion was fortunate to survive.

There was little comfort for the sick. Colonel Wayne informed the Pennsylvania Committee of Safety the condition of the men was "Shocking to Humanity & beggars all description. We have neither Beds or Bedding for our Sick to Lay on or under other than their own thin wretched Cloathing no Medicine or Regimen Suteable for them, the Dead & Dying lying mingled together." His lieutenant colonel wrote home after a visit to the hospital that conditions "can not be viewed in any milder light than black murder." He sadly added, "If you was here, your heart would melt."

The men endeavored to keep themselves entertained. "Cards and drinking are the diversions which the whole garrison are daily employed at," wrote Elmer. Consumption of alcohol was always a recreation in the American army during the Revolution. In fact, it was more than that, as the men expected rum as part of their rations. For those relegated to standing guard outside the time was lengthy and boring. Wayne attempted to ease the pain of the exposure to cold by ordering each sentry to consume a gill (four ounces) of rum before going outside.

While the rank and file favored rum, the officers often imbibed wine. In a letter to his friend Sharp Delany, Wayne described the frigid cold and his prescribed cure. "Last night has frozen Lake Champlain to the Centre," he wrote. "Our poor fellows severely felt the Effect of it—for my own part I was so Congeal'd that after turning before the fire for three hours…I was not half thawed until I put one Bottle of wine under my Sword Belt at Dinner."

On January 1, 1777, Elmer and 20 men were assigned to the surviving gondola, the *New York*, which was locked in the ice and had a shelter covering the open deck. The space was far too small and Elmer sent most of the men back to their barracks. He then took up quarters aboard the row-galley *Gates*. When Wayne visited the *Gates*, he found no sentry. "He damned all our souls to hell," Elmer recorded. "But my great consolation is, that the power thereof is not in his hands, blessed be God for it."

The men continued to parade on the ice. On January 9, they went through "sundry manœvers" for two or three hours. Three days later, they drilled from 2 p.m. until it was "quite dark." On January 16 during a snowstorm, Elmer's men paraded at the Mount Independence barracks, but did not go out on the ice as ordered. The next day they spent nearly four hours on the lake.

These creepers allowed a soldier to keep his footing on the ice.

A wine bottle found by underwater archaeologists.

A LONG, BITTER WINTER

A memorial to the soldiers buried on the Mount was erected by the local chapter of the Daughters of the American Revolution in 1908.

On December 21, the garrison had totaled 2,384 men. Two Massachusetts militia regiments arrived, but many more men left. In Wayne's phrase, "the Eastern people [were] Running away in the Clouds of the Night—(some before and all soon as their time expires)." But Yankees were not the only ones counting the days until they could leave. On February 11, Wayne clashed with Captain John Nelson's Rifle Company, a Pennsylvania unit that had earlier served in Wayne's own regiment. The men believed their enlistments had expired and were ready to march for home. Confronting this mutiny, Wayne pointed his pistol at a sergeant and ordered the company to put down their weapons. The sergeant fell to his knees, begging for his life, and the rest of the men grounded their muskets. In the end, they agreed to remain nine more days.

After the departure of the three Pennsylvania battalions and Burrall's Regiment in late January and early February, the entire garrison numbered less than 1,200. Wayne complained that the men he had were "Children, twelve or fifteen years of age In time they'l make good men—as yet they are too young."

As winter progressed, exercises on the ice stopped, but death remained a constant. "The men died so fast for some time that the living grew quite wearied in digging graves for the dead in this rocky, frozen ground," Elmer wrote in February. On one occasion, the New Jersey men dug two graves, but before they could carry the bodies to the graveyard, Pennsylvanians appropriated the holes for their dead. "A wrangle between the two parties ensued" before the New Jersey men evicted the dead Pennsylvanians.

The New Jersey men waited anxiously for the arrival of new troops to relieve them. "You must certainly suppose our Hearts are in Jersey, tho' our Bodies are on Mt Independence," Lieutenant Colonel Francis Barber wrote to Colonel Dayton, who was in Morristown. Finally, Colonel Pierce Long's New Hampshire militia began to arrive, a few at a time. Wayne told an embarrassed lieutenant, Ezekiel Worthen, "He never knew a Regiment marched in such a d____ manner."

On March 2, the Third New Jersey at last left Mount Independence. "Just as the drums beat the assembly I paraded the men," wrote Elmer, "and as soon as the baggage was all packed up, without eating one mouthful, set out on the march with our men . . . and proceeded up the Lake towards Skeenesborough on the slippery road."

It had been a long, hard winter at the Lake Champlain forts. No official account is available totaling the number of soldiers who succumbed to the freezing temperatures, disease, and insufficient supplies of food and clothing, but dozens and perhaps even hundreds were buried at Ticonderoga and Mount Independence in December, January, and February.

With the onset of March, the weather began to improve, and Jeduthan Baldwin had returned from his leave with a new set of orders for further transforming Mount Independence.

Camp Followers and Ladies

Women always played an important role in eighteenth-century armies. As camp followers, they cooked, sewed, washed clothes, and nursed the sick. They "followed" their husbands with their children and lived the same rough life as soldiers, but only occasionally do the day-to-day details of their lives survive in the written record.

In July 1776, women were "draughted" to nurse the sick at Fort George and promised the "customary allowance of provision." Anthony Wayne was strict in his orders on December 10, 1776: "Any Woman belonging to the Regt, who shall refuse to wash for the Men, shall be immediately drumm'd out of the Regt, as they are not found in Victuals to distress and render the Men unfit for Duty, but to keep them clean and decent."

On June 29, 1777, as the Americans prepared to face Burgoyne's invasion, Timothy Ryne of Ebenezer Francis's Regiment was tried "for rushing into the tent of Joel Pringle [of Warner's Regiment] and offering abuse to said Pringle's wife." No details were recorded; Ryne was found guilty and sentenced to 70 lashes.

Surgeon James Thacher described the retreat from Mount Independence by boat. "Our fleet consisted of five armed gallies and two hundred bateaux and boats deeply laden with cannon, tents, provisions, invalids and women."

Only occasionally did the wives of officers stay at the Lake Champlain forts. Margaret Hay, wife of deputy commissary general Udney Hay, wintered at Ticonderoga in 1776-1777 and in the evenings

Frederika Charlotte Louise von Massow, the Baroness von Riedesel. Riedesel, Letters and Journal Relating to the War of the American Revolution and the Capture of the Germans Troops at Saratoga *(1867)*

played cards with the ranking officers. They formed "a very intimate club," noted Lieutenant Ebenezer Elmer jealously from the Mount Independence side of the lake. When Mrs. Hay left for Albany on April 14, Jeduthan Baldwin, General Wayne, and others accompanied her to Lake George Landing.

Archaeologists have found no distinctive material culture relating to women on Mount Independence, which is not surprising. Perhaps a ceramic plate suggests a woman's presence, perhaps not. Historians know the most about the aristocratic women who accompanied Burgoyne's army in 1777.

Lady Harriet Acland was the wife of Major John Dyke Acland, who was wounded at Hubbardton. At Mount Independence she nursed him back to health. After he was wounded and captured at the Second Battle of Saratoga, she crossed enemy lines at night to be at his side.

A camp follower. Gary Zaboly / Mount Independence Coalition

Frederika Charlotte Louise von Massow, the Baroness von Riedesel, kept a diary, which is one of the most readable accounts of Burgoyne's campaign. The Generalin Riedesel (Mrs. General in a nineteenth-century translation) was among the most courageous figures in the army. In a cellar in Saratoga, she saw to her three daughters, frightened women, and wounded officers. Eleven cannonballs crashed through the house. "We could plainly hear them rolling over our heads," she wrote.

On October 17, 1777, Burgoyne's army marched in surrender by the ranks of silent Americans. Three thousand British came first, then 2,400 Germans, then nearly 300 women. These were the camp followers, who like their American sisters, washed, cooked, and nursed.

CHAPTER FIVE

Plans, Politics, and Preparations

"Mount Independence is by much the most defensible, and may be made a post capable of sustaining a long and vigorous siege."

— PHILIP SCHUYLER TO ARTHUR ST. CLAIR, JUNE 5, 1777

On November 2, 1776, the day before it was certain the British were withdrawing from Crown Point, a congressional delegation reached Ticonderoga. Richard Stockton, a New Jersey aristocrat, and George Clymer, a Philadelphia merchant, were on what today would be called a fact-finding mission. Before they arrived, they saw the Third Jersey, Ebenezer Elmer's regiment, marching from Fort Stanwix (Fort Schuyler) to Lake Champlain and were shocked at how poorly equipped the men were for cold weather. Stockton told a fellow New Jersey congressman he would give away every pair of stockings in his baggage, "but this is a drop of water in the ocean."

At Fort George, Stockton and Clymer tried to purchase straw so that men in the hospital would not have to lie on bare boards, and they wished for "good female Nurses." Among their first recommendations to Congress was that a new General Hospital be built on Mount Independence, "Fort George being at much too great a Distance."

Once at Lake Champlain, they interviewed or gathered written statements from Gates, Baldwin, artillery Captain Ebenezer Stevens, and other officers, doctors, commissary officials, and potential contractors. Gates was blunt in his comments: "I am almost tired of applying to Congress for supplies. They mean to do right; but besides their labouring under very great

On a fine day in March 1777, Americans work on the Great Bridge from Mount Independence to Ticonderoga.
Gary Zaboly /
Mount Independence Coalition

A portrait of Brigadier General Enoch Poor of New Hampshire, drawn by Polish engineer Thaddeus Kosciuszko. It is said that Kosciuszko sketched Poor while in church at Valley Forge.
New Hampshire Historical Society

Opposite page: A map drawn by British Lieutenant Charles Wintersmith, showing the fortifications on Mount Independence by the summer of 1777.
John Carter Brown Library at Brown University

difficulties to supply in due time the demands of their Generals, they certainly want judicious, and very often disinterested information."

The list of needs was monumental: 20 iron 18-pound cannons, 10 brass howitzers, 2,000 spades, 2,000 shovels, 3,000 felling axes, 800,000 ten-penny nails, window glass for the barracks, two floating gun platforms, and on and on. With winter descending, the committee recommended that vegetables and "antiscorbutics" be sent north to prevent scurvy, which "is apt to be fatal there." Schuyler listed "woolen Caps" from Philadelphia.

In his planning, Baldwin counted on 10,000 men to work on the fortifications and to man the lines. He proposed building a stronger fort on Mount Independence with four bastions (projecting fortifications) and a covert or covered way on the east and south sides, which would allow entrenched soldiers to be positioned outside the fort. He wanted to turn the earthen Citadel into a redoubt and to repair old Fort Ticonderoga with stone and lime. Then, significantly, he added, "build a Block-house on the southwest Hill across the Lake." This hill, known as the Sugar Loaf, Sugar Hill, or Mount Defiance, rises 750 feet above the lake and it loomed above the American defenses, particularly on the Ticonderoga side.

Schuyler, who was as much a politician as a general, suspected that it was unlikely Congress and the states would again send 10,000 men to Lake Champlain. He had always believed that Mount Independence had the potential to stand alone. "The fortifications at Ticonderoga should be as much contracted as possible," he told Stockton and Clymer. A new fort should be built "on Mount Independence, to cover batteries near the lake side and the redoubt on the Ticonderoga side, so as that the Pass [narrows on Lake Champlain] may be defended by a few men." He hoped for provisions to support 5,000 men for eight months.

He suggested a line of caissons be sunk across the lake at the narrowest point to obstruct the passage of British vessels. Such underwater crib-like structures holding *chevaux-de-frise* or spikes were being used in the Delaware River south of Philadelphia to block British ships. A young Polish engineer, Thaddeus Kosciuszko, was overseeing those defenses. In Schuyler's plan, the caissons would rise above the water and be connected to form a permanent bridge. On December 28, Congress, meeting in Baltimore, took up Stockton and Clymer's report and approved sunken caissons, floating gun platforms, and measures to prevent scurvy.

While Schuyler remained commander of the Northern Department, Gates followed Congress to Baltimore in order to request an independent command. Congress, especially the New Englanders, had

In a close-up from the Wintersmith map, the Great Bridge ties together the fortifications on both sides of Lake Champlain.
John Carter Brown Library at Brown University

been feuding with Schuyler since the campaign in Canada. Gates's lobbying efforts were eventually rewarded when Hancock ordered him to Ticonderoga "to take the Command of the Army in that Department," but the orders did not indicate whether Schuyler was being relieved of command. In fact, the resolution did not mention Schuyler at all. Nevertheless, Gates proceeded to Albany assuming he had been given command of the Northern Department. Meanwhile, uncertain of his status in the army, Schuyler traveled to Philadelphia to reclaim his seat in the Continental Congress.

On March 1, Baldwin began work on the 1,600-foot-long Great Bridge from Ticonderoga to Mount Independence. The previous November he had sounded the channel, so he knew how tall each caisson needed to be. The bridge would require 22 of these piers, about 50 feet apart, rising 10 feet above the water. The piers were to be topped with a 14-foot-wide plank road.

Although not all the details of construction are understood, documents and archaeological evidence suggest the method. Men built the caissons in holes cut in the ice, row upon row like a sinking log cabin. Guided by pilings and weighted with stones as ballast, the caissons sank into the water. The tallest piers were 40 feet in height before they went through the layer of mud and were solidly on the bottom. The work pro-

gressed quickly at first. March 8 was "a fine Day at ye Bridge." By March 9, ten caissons were sunk in the lake. But within a few days the ice was "very Roten," and Baldwin turned to other projects. On paper he designed the new fort. Under his supervision, men completed a blockhouse near old Fort Ticonderoga, cut timber for the General Hospital, and repaired the floating bridge. Projects included a "house to boil soap and make candles" and a bake house.

Winter had offered the forts some protection. Now men began to calculate that the wide lake to the north would be navigable by the second week in April. Anthony Wayne begged Schuyler "to rouse the public officers in those States [New England] from their shameful lethargy before it be too late. I do assure you there is not one moment to spare in bringing in troops and the necessary supplies."

Warming weather brought raiding parties. At Sabbath Day Point on the west shore of Lake George, Kahnawake Mohawks commanded by a Loyalist captain surprised a sleeping New York ranger company, killing at least four men and capturing about 20, who were taken to Canada as prisoners.

With the ice gone, work on the Great Bridge changed. Piers were begun near shore and then floated into place and sunk. Oxen were few; the forage to feed them was scarce, so manpower hauled many of the giant logs and the tons of ballast. On March 26,

With no more than logs and stone, the Americans worked to bridge the quarter mile from Mount Independence to Ticonderoga.

In the late 20th century, it took heavy equipment to move the logs of the Great Bridge. In 1777, the work was done by oxen and manpower. Vermont Division for Historic Preservation

one pier fell apart. The next day the bottom of another collapsed. A month later, a third flipped over. Then during a Sunday sermon, a storm broke the floating bridge and boom, and men rushed to maneuver them back into place.

Undaunted, Baldwin calmly recorded these setbacks without additional comment and continued with his many projects. In early April he "laid out a large gardin" on the flat, tillable land along the lake southwest of the Grand Battery. Later in the month, he began construction of a crane at the edge of the cliff above Catfish Bay so that supplies could be raised by block and tackle to the plateau and the Star Fort. Much of the time, he was on the Ticonderoga side constructing redoubts and blockhouses.

Wayne finally left Ticonderoga on April 29 for Washington's army and command of the Pennsylvania Line, leaving John Paterson of Massachusetts as commander for the next three weeks. Gates was still in Albany, commanding via correspondence but offering no written directions on which of the countless projects should be given priority. Schuyler, by then a congressman, continued to push for adoption of his original plan—build a barrier bridge, contract the Ticonderoga lines, strengthen Mount Independence, and control Lake George by building a fleet. Accordingly, at the end of April, Congress passed a resolution allowing Gates to employ "his whole force to the strengthening and securing Fort Independence and the water defence of Lake George." But Gates apparently did not agree with Schuyler's strategy. He replied to Congress: "I see no Reason for abandoning any part of the post of Ticonderoga…I believe, that Ticonderoga may be as safe this year, as it was the Last."

With spring came fresh Continental regiments, five from Massachusetts and three from New Hampshire. But they were poorly supplied and equipped. Wayne told Goose Van Schaick, commander at Fort George, that many new recruits did not have muskets and he was forced to arm a quarter of them with spears. Colonel Thomas Marshall of Massachusetts, whose regiment was in the barracks of the Star Fort, complained that men going on a scout needed to borrow shoes from those who remained in camp. He told Gates his men did not have the "cloathing to appear decent in." They had expected to be supplied once they reached the forts. Quartermaster Lieutenant Colonel Udney Hay pointed out the troops needed cooking pots and tents.

Caissons of the Great Bridge still rise above the mud at the bottom of Lake Champlain. Occasionally, a massive timber surfaces, as this one did in 1991. Preserved, it is now in the museum in the Mount Independence Visitor Center. Vermont Division for Historic Preservation

Despite the hardships of camp life, springtime on Lake Champlain had advantages. In his journal Baldwin confessed, "Drank Tea Punch & wine at Mr. Adamses & live as gayly as if danger was at a distance." Ducks were early visitors and supplemented the monotonous diet. Vast flocks of passenger pigeons came through in May. Men were frenzied in their attempt to kill the birds, which could be fried or thrown into the stew kettle. Moses Greenleaf, a lieutenant in Ebenezer Francis's Regiment, "catch'd" 20 dozen in a single day. The fishing along East Creek was good. Lotteries offered the chance to win cash. For three days in a row in early June, men on the Ticonderoga side "played ball."

On May 5, Baldwin staked out the new General Hospital, located where the road from Catfish Bay reached the plateau. The hospital was to be 250 feet long, 25 feet wide, and two stories tall, accommodating as many as 600 patients. Four stone fireplaces were to heat the building.

On May 12, Polish engineer Thaddeus Kosciuszko reached Ticonderoga. Gates told Paterson, "When he has thoroughly made himself acquainted with the works, [I] have ordered him to point out to you, where and in what manner the best improvements and additions can be made thereto." Kosciuszko was not meant to replace Baldwin, Gates stressed, but to serve him. At first Kosciuszko developed plans for the Ticonderoga side, which he sent to Gates in French. "We are very fond here of making Block houses and they are erected in the most improper places," he wrote in the translation that Gates read. He told Gates that if his plan was adopted, "I say the Enemy cannot hurt us. We have an excellent place not only to resist the Enemy, but beat them." However, Kosciuszko's drawing of his proposed works does not survive, so it is impossible to know exactly what he was thinking.

On May 28, Gates wrote to Baldwin that he had adopted Kosciuszko's design and recommended "the utmost harmony" between the two men. Baldwin was to concentrate on the bridge and Mount Independence, while Kosciuszko oversaw the Ticonderoga side.

On June 3, Schuyler returned to Albany carrying orders from the Continental Congress. He was again (or had been all along) commander of the Northern Department, which included Ticonderoga and Mount Independence, making Gates his subordinate. Gates was surprised by his fall from power. He remained commander of the Lake Champlain forts, but, in Schuyler's understated words, he showed "a Disinclination to continue to serve in this Department." Outraged, Gates rushed to Philadelphia to make his case before Congress.

Schuyler ordered St. Clair, now a major general, to Lake Champlain "with all convenient speed." The entire Northern Army was not large enough to man the far-reaching works on both sides of the lake, he told him. "As Mount Independence is by much the most defensible, and may be made a post capable of sustaining a long and vigorous siege, it is my intention that your first care should be to bestow the utmost attention to fortifying the Mount."

An International Hero

Thaddeus (Tadeusz) Kosciuszko (1746-1817) is a hero in Poland, where he led the struggle for human rights and for freedom from Russia, and in Belarus, where his birthplace is located. His statue stands in Cracow and Lodz; on the grounds of West Point; and in major U.S. cities including Washington, Boston, Philadelphia, and Chicago. Thomas Jefferson wrote, "He is as pure a son of liberty, as I have ever known, and of that liberty which is to go to all, and not to the few or the rich alone."

Kosciuszko, then 30, arrived in Philadelphia in the late summer of 1776. At the time, Congress was overwhelmed by foreigners with exaggerated credentials, but the young Pole, trained in Warsaw and Paris, wanted to contribute his engineering expertise to the American cause. He directed the construction of defenses on the Delaware River, including underwater *chevaux-de-frise* [spikes] held by caissons similar to those of the Great Bridge between Mount Independence and Ticonderoga.

In the spring of 1777, he was sent to Lake Champlain by Horatio Gates to point out "where and in what manner the best improvements and additions can be made." Kosciuszko found himself in the middle of the debate on how to defend two sides of the lake. He sent Gates a revised plan, but wrote (in French) that he did not want to proceed before Gates arrived. "I will give you the reason, I love peace & to be on good terms with all the world if possible." He said he would "return home & plant Cabbages" before he would confront the officers at the lake. As General Burgoyne approached, Kosciuszko oversaw the construction of defenses on the southeast of Mount Independence.

Kosciuszko's greatest contributions to American independence came later. He designed the fortifications on Bemis Heights that stopped Burgoyne and led to the victory at Saratoga as well as those at West Point, the key to the Hudson River. As Nathanael Greene's chief engineer in the Carolinas, he was instrumental in the campaign that exhausted Cornwallis and led to the British surrender at Yorktown.

The young Thaddeus Kosciuszko.
Courtesy Brest Regional Museum of Local Lore, Belarus

CHAPTER SIX

General Arthur St. Clair's Predicament

"If the enemy intend to attack us, I assure you, sir, we are very ill-prepared to receive them."

— Arthur St. Clair to Philip Schuyler, June 13, 1777

In the rain on June 12, 1777, Major General Arthur St. Clair sailed the length of Lake George to assume command at Ticonderoga. He was 40, born in Thurso in the far northeast of Scotland. He pronounced his name *Sinclair*, which is how his father and his aristocratic relatives, the earls of Caithness, spelled it. Much about his early life is uncertain, but after the French and Indian War he married a young woman with a fortune and became a man of property and position on the western Pennsylvania frontier. Like Anthony Wayne, who was his rival among ambitious Pennsylvania officers, St. Clair would rather have been

The strength of General John Burgoyne's invasion in the summer of 1777 is captured in this illustration for a 1998 article in Smithsonian *magazine. Greg Harlin / Collection of Mount Independence State Historic Site*

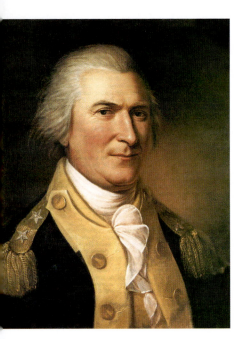

Major General Arthur St. Clair, the last American commander of Mount Independence.
Charles Willson Peale / Independence National Historical Park

leading troops in George Washington's army, preparing to meet Sir William Howe.

When news of a springtime threat on Lake Champlain reached Philadelphia, Congress ordered him north "without delay." But the first alarm vanished quickly. Congress and Washington were certain that most of the British and German troops in Canada would be sent by sea to New York to strengthen Howe's army. "No serious attempt would be made upon Ticonderoga; at most it would be a diversion only," Hancock told St. Clair. Lake Champlain seemed to be so secure that St. Clair brought along his 11-year-old son Art.

St. Clair spent several days in Albany meeting with Gates and Kosciuszko. Although he did not receive written orders from Gates, he was told to implement Kosciuszko's plan for the Ticonderoga side of the lake. Then, as St. Clair was preparing to leave Albany for Lake Champlain, Philip Schuyler resumed command and gave him exacting written orders to concentrate his efforts on strengthening Mount Independence. As St. Clair rode north, he was accompanied by Richard Varick, deputy commissary general of musters and Schuyler's trusted aide, and Brigadier General Matthias Alexis Roche de Fermoy, a French soldier of fortune from Martinique in the Caribbean, who would play a small but significant role in the events that would unfold less than a month later.

On the day St. Clair arrived at Ticonderoga, two men from Canada were brought to headquarters by scouts. These prisoners freely stated that General John Burgoyne was organizing a campaign aimed at the Lake Champlain forts and that he would arrive with an army of 10,000 in less than two weeks. A smaller detachment would advance from the west along the Mohawk River. St. Clair was incredulous. He concluded that one of the men, William Amsbury, was a spy, spreading misinformation designed to intimidate the garrison. When Washington heard the news in a letter from Schuyler, he agreed: "Supposing the plan mentioned in Amsbury's evidence to be true, I cannot conceive that it will be in the power of the Enemy to carry it into execution." He was convinced the American position was sufficiently strong "to hold it against any attack."

As he assessed the situation, St. Clair quickly learned how weak the forts actually were. He told Schuyler in his first letter, "If the enemy intend to attack us, I assure you, sir, we are very ill-prepared to receive them." He calculated that fewer than 1,600 Continental troops were fit for duty. The Hampshire County, Massachusetts, militia, who were "engaged for no particular term … go off whenever they please." The tents were bad; there were no oxen; moisture was ruining the gunpowder; and provisions were so scarce that reinforcements from the militia could not be fed.

St. Clair told friend and Continental Congressman James Wilson about the poor state of the fortifications: "They are much worse than when I left them [the previous November], a very strong abatis, in which the security of Mount Independence chiefly consisted, having been almost entirely burned up in the winter, and a great part of the breastwork destroyed."

Varick also reported on the condition of the forts: "Very little has been done to make Mount Independance defensible. ... [T]he Time of the Troops has been taken up in raising Redoubts & Works between the Old Fort & French Lines & in Making Defences at the Lines to prevent their Rear being attacked." When Varick inspected the regiments, he described men without uniforms and "Many Very Young Lads, Some of whom I have rejected & many others had not the Situation of our Garrison forbid the Measure."

With St. Clair's arrival, regional and personal rivalries intensified. The change in command was a "Mortifying Stroke" to the many Gates supporters among the officers, Varick wrote. He blamed Yankees for much that was wrong. "Were New Englandmen to be at War half a Century their Troops would not be disciplined under Officers from their own States," he told Schuyler.

The garrison was gripped with fear of Indians. On June 17, a few unarmed men going fishing within sight of the French Lines were attacked. Two were killed, two more taken prisoner, and rescuers suffered more casualties. The same day a party of Whitcomb's Rangers and volunteers from other regiments returned to the forts, having been ambushed between Ticonderoga and Crown Point. Then there was a brief lull, and St. Clair hoped that "the Indians said to be about us were ... the children of a disturbed imagination."

From the first—perhaps from the summer of 1776—St. Clair doubted Schuyler's plan to make Mount Independence the focal point of the defenses. On June 18 he put his arguments in writing. He was "making some improvements on the Mount," he told Schuyler, but the two sides of the lake were so interdependent, "it will be very dangerous to give up either, and yet it is certain we can not, with our present numbers, hold both." He would defend Ticonderoga "as long as possible" before retreating.

Alarmed by St. Clair's reports, Schuyler arrived on June 18 to inspect the situation for himself. At a council of war two days later, St. Clair again expressed doubt about Mount Independence withstanding a siege. But after discussion, Schuyler, St. Clair, and the three brigadier generals signed a unanimous statement that ratified Schuyler's views. They agreed a garrison of fewer than 2,500 effective rank-and-file soldiers was "greatly inadequate to the defense of both posts." They decided that if one side of the lake had to be abandoned, it ought to be Ticonderoga. Unnecessary artillery and supplies should be moved to Mount Independence "without delay." But the lines and fortifications on the Mount were "very deficient" and "repairing the old, and adding new works, ought to claim immediate attention." If more provisions did not arrive, it would be "prudent to provide for a retreat" by repairing bateaux and hauling others across the portage from Lake George.

Archaeologists discovered the base of an H-shaped, double-sided fireplace in the center of the American blockhouse above the Southern Battery. Mount Independence State Historic Site photo

A plan of a blockhouse from Thomas Anburey's Travels through the Interior Parts of America *(1789).*

The Mount Independence Cannon

The 9-foot, 11-inch cannon displayed at the Mount Independence Historic Site was forged in England in the mid-1670s and raised from Lake Champlain in the summer of 1993. The gun is referred to as a light 12-pounder, meaning that it could hurl a 12-pound cannonball more than a mile. "Light" is relative: the gun weighs 3,124 pounds.

Through the markings on the barrel and careful British Admiralty record keeping, much is known of the early history of the cannon. It was forged in Horsmonden in the district of Kent by His Majesty's Gunfounder John Browne Jr. and delivered to the Woolrich Dockyard on the Thames in the summer of 1676, a century before the American Revolution. At the time, it was a state-of-the-art weapon, a Rupertinoe gun. Although the exact process of heating and cooling in founding the gun is a mystery, the result was a strong, durable, and lighter cannon.

From 1679 to 1736, it was aboard the *HMS Essex*, which at first carried 70 guns. The *Essex* sailed the north and south Atlantic oceans, the Mediterranean and Baltic seas, and the Caribbean, and for a time, served as a fleet flagship. After the ship was dismantled, the Mount Independence cannon was used on land, a common practice with aging cannon.

The history of the cannon ashore calls for some speculation. Most likely the gun was sent to America during the French and Indian War and seized by Americans near New York early in the Revolution. It was taken to Lake Champlain in the winter of 1776-1777. Then it was abandoned on shore by the retreating Americans on July 6, 1777, and dropped in the lake by the British, who had more time to burn and destroy fortifications on Mount Independence before their retreat on November 8, 1777. One trunnion, a pivot on the gun carriage, was knocked off, rendering the cannon useless.

In the summers of 1992-1993, the Lake Champlain Maritime Museum, which was hired by the Vermont Division of Historic Preservation, conducted an underwater survey at Mount Independence's northern point. During the first year, the cannon was discovered off the shore of Mount Independence in about eight feet of water. It was raised the following summer. Scott McLaughlin researched the gun for his 2000 master's thesis at Texas A&M University.

Photo: Vermont Division for Historic Preservation

The Mount Independence cannon was raised from Lake Champlain in the summer of 1993. It and a wheel can be seen in the historic site's museum.

On the same day as the council, Kosciuszko and Baldwin began supervising the construction of three cannon batteries on the southeast of Mount Independence, where the peninsula was most vulnerable. Five to six hundred men were on fatigue duty from 6 a.m. to 6 p.m., digging, moving rock, and cutting abatis. Although the hill rose steeply from the neck of land between East Creek and the lake to the south, if an attacker flanked the Mount on the eastern side and gained the plateau, the advantage would shift.

The next day cannon were moved from Ticonderoga to the wharf at the southern end of Mount Independence, where they could be hauled up the hill to the new batteries. When St. Clair visited the Mount, he gave orders that the old hospital inside the picket fort be turned into a laboratory for munitions, replacing a less secure facility outside the walls. Soon Baldwin was overseeing the driving of logs into the mud in East Creek to stop enemy boats from reaching the neck of land.

On June 27, St. Clair wrote a letter to Gates filled with pessimism. Mount Independence had been "almost totally neglected," he wrote, but was now the last resort. "I am pretty certain I am in a Situation where I have no Prospect of doing much Service to my Country and have Captivity or Death before my Eyes." But despite his private assessment, by the end of June the Mount had stopped being an afterthought and was again the foundation upon which the defense of Lake Champlain rested.

Today the site of the crane provides a beautiful overlook of Catfish Bay.

As the Americans labored to prepare for attack, the generals still did not believe that the British threat was serious. On June 25, Schuyler wrote to Congress from his home in Saratoga (present-day Schuylerville) that he hoped to repulse the enemy "should they attempt a real attack, which I conjecture will not be soon, if at all."

But Schuyler's news was already out of date. On June 23 a scout returned to the forts with word the British had reached Gilliland's Creek (today's Bouquet River at Willsboro, New York), 40 miles north. The next day another scout reported seven ships lying off Crown Point and troops landing at Chimney Point. On Thursday, June 26, between the mills on the La Chute River and Lake George Landing, Indians killed two men, captured two others, and left two more wounded. "The Scene thickens fast," St. Clair reported to Schuyler, "and Sunday next, it seems, is fixed for the attack on this place." Indians were so active that even Benjamin Whitcomb's best scouts found it difficult to get close enough to Burgoyne's army to bring back dependable intelligence.

Still, St. Clair was uncertain. On June 28 he wrote,

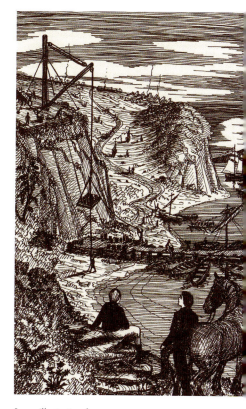

In an illustration for Independence Must Be Won, *a 1964 novel for young people written by Phillip Viereck, illustrator Ellen Viereck depicted the crane that hoisted supplies from Catfish Bay to the height of the Mount.*
Ellen Viereck / Collection of the Mount Independence Historic Site

The Southern Battery dominates the flat land to the south and east of Mount Independence

"I conclude they are either in full force or very weak, and hope, by letting loose the Indians, to intimidate us. I incline to believe the last." Later in the day, three scouts brought a largely accurate report: 8,000 Regulars, plus 1,500 Canadians and Indians (an exaggeration), were camped at Putnam's Point, less than 10 miles away. In the morning, St. Clair took the precaution of sending off his son under the care of Richard Varick.

At noon on July 1, the American garrison fired 13 cannon to celebrate the news that the British had abandoned New Jersey, but St. Clair was concerned the enemy would sense the weakness of the garrison and ordered the soldiers not to fire their muskets. As the heavy guns thundered from the fortifications, enemy bateaux appeared off Three Mile Point and crossed the lake to the east side. Through his spyglass, St. Clair counted and estimated: 41 bateaux, perhaps 20 men in each. He believed they were "foreigners," part of Burgoyne's German contingent, undoubtedly aiming to cut the military road and come at the Mount from land.

Before daylight on July 2, St. Clair sent orders to burn everything at Lake George Landing that could not be carried away. The smoke at the landing and the mills along the river alerted the enemy. A British detachment under Brigadier General Simon Fraser seized the fort on Mount Hope, while Captain Alexander Fraser, Simon's nephew, advanced to cut the major supply route from Lake George.

Between one and two o'clock in the afternoon, in a skirmish outside the French Lines, five or six men from Francis's and Warner's regiments were killed and another 10 wounded. After volleys were fired from the French Lines, the Americans captured a sergeant, plied him with rum, and learned the true size of Burgoyne's force.

On July 1, by his own records, Burgoyne had a force of 3,724 rank-and-file British Regulars, 3,016 German rank and file, 250 Canadians and provincials, and 400 Indians. Add officers, sergeants, artillerymen, musicians, chaplains, and surgeons, and Burgoyne's army exceeded 9,000 men. He had brought 138 cannon to break Ticonderoga and Mount Independence.

St. Clair, who later admitted to underestimating the size of his own force, believed he had no more than 2,089 "effectives, rank and file," but taking into account men who were recovering from sickness, most often measles, and those assigned to fatigue duty, the Americans likely had 3,000 foot soldiers on July 1.

On July 3, as both sides prepared for a siege, Colonel Seth Warner of Vermont and Colonel Benjamin Bellows of New Hampshire led eight to nine hundred militiamen on to Mount Independence. They drove with them at least 40 head of cattle (Baldwin believed 80) and a flock of sheep. "A fine reinforcement at this Time when we are surrounded by our enemy, which I pray God may be scattered," Baldwin wrote in his journal.

John Burgoyne: An Overconfident General

John Burgoyne (1722-1792) was a gambler, womanizer, playwright, Member of Parliament, and innovative commander. He gained his early fame in a lightning cavalry attack to capture the Spanish town of Valencia de Alcántara and believed that boldness, speed, and surprise were his strengths. He encouraged his officers to educate themselves, to show initiative, and to treat enlisted men with more humanity than was common in the eighteenth century.

In England in the winter of 1776-1777, Burgoyne argued that Governor-General Guy Carleton should have pressed his advantage after the Battle of Valcour Island. He sent Lord George Germain, secretary of state for the American colonies, a lengthy plan, "Thoughts for Conducting the War from This Side of Canada."

Burgoyne proposed leading an army south on Lake Champlain and the upper Hudson River, while a second force advanced from the west on the Mohawk River to Albany. Meanwhile, Commander in Chief William Howe's army would sail north on the Hudson. A three-pronged attack was not original with Burgoyne, but he showed he had mastered the details and had the drive to carry it out. "I do not conceive that any expedition from the sea can be so formidable to the enemy, or so effectual to close the war, as an invasion from Canada by Ticonderoga. This last measure ought not to be thought of, but upon positive conviction of its necessity," he wrote.

The general was so confident of his success that on Christmas Day 1776 he bet his friend Charles Fox, an outspoken opponent of the war, "one pony [50 guineas] that he will be home victorious from America by Christmas Day, 1777."

But Burgoyne's supposed strengths turned into weaknesses. His rapid victory at Ticonderoga and Mount Independence made him overconfident. He was convinced the Americans had "no men of military science" and so marched obstinately south. Finally in mid-September he crossed the Hudson to Philip Schuyler's Saratoga and then broke up the floating bridge. His army was cut off from supplies, and many men were sick with dysentery. The expedition on the Mohawk had been stopped. Howe was not coming north on the Hudson. And Albany was still 35 miles away.

"The English never lose ground," Baroness Riedesel remembered Burgoyne as saying. Briefly she "cherished the sweet hope of sure victory." Many histories quote a more theatrical version: "Britons never retreat."

Lieutenant General John Burgoyne.
Sir Joshua Reynolds/The Frick Collection

64 STRONG GROUND

CHAPTER SEVEN

A Controversial Retreat

"The evacuation of Ticonderoga and Mount Independence is an event of chagrin and surprise not apprehended nor within the compass of my reasoning."

— George Washington to Philip Schuyler, July 15, 1777

On the afternoon of July 3, British Brigadier General Simon Fraser sent a party of light infantry to explore the prominent mountain south of Ticonderoga known locally as Sugar Hill. The next day, Fraser, a Scottish highlander in his late forties, climbed the mountain himself and gave orders "to use every possible expedition" to haul two medium 12-pounders to the summit, followed by howitzers and 24-pounders. He expected the first battery to be operational by the evening of July 6. In a letter to a friend, Fraser quoted a "sagacious Indian," who asked, "If the great father of the sun had created [the hill] lately, as

British cannon are ready to open fire from towering Mount Defiance. Greg Harlin for Smithsonian *magazine Collection of the Mount Independence State Historic Site*

in the various contests about possessing Ticonderoga … it never occurred to any person to occupy it before we did."

Around noon on July 5, Lieutenant Moses Greenleaf of Francis's Regiment, who had been dining with fellow officers, noticed soldiers at work atop Sugar Hill, sometimes called Mount Defiance. Baldwin recognized that the British were building a gun battery.

The prospect of cannon upon Mount Defiance joined a cascade of bad news for the Americans. In the preceding days, elements of Burgoyne's German contingent had been slowly but steadily advancing southward on the lake's eastern shore toward Mount Independence, hacking their way through virgin forest amid clouds of mosquitoes, eventually taking up a position on East Creek directly across from the Mount. Once this force managed to find a way across or around the marshy creek, they could cut the military road, blocking the Americans' retreat by land.

On the Ticonderoga side, seven British regiments plus light infantry (skirmishers), elite grenadiers, two British artillery brigades, and Wilhelm von Gall's Erbprinz Regiment, had sealed off the peninsula. Heavy guns were being positioned less than three-quarters of a mile from the French Lines. These guns, combined with those in batteries being constructed by the Germans on the eastern shore, together with the ones on Mount Defiance, put the Ticonderoga defenses in the middle of a deadly crossfire.

Soon after the discovery that the enemy was putting cannon atop Defiance, General St. Clair called a council of general officers. "The Batteries of the Enemy are ready to open upon the Ticonderoga Side," he told them, "and the camp is very much exposed to their Fire, and to be enfiladed on all quarters; and there is also reason to expect an attack upon Ticonderoga and Mount Independence at the same time, in which case neither could draw any support from the other."

Step by step he led them to a decision to retreat. First, the council unanimously decided to transfer all troops to Mount Independence during the night of July 5-6 and to carry over the remaining cannon and supplies, if possible. Then St. Clair asked whether Mount Independence could be defended or should the army retreat into the countryside. The neck of land and the narrow water route to Skenesborough would soon be cut off, isolating Mount Independence from supplies and reinforcements. The council resolved to retreat "as soon as possible, and that we shall be very fortunate to effect it."

General Schuyler had not foreseen guns on Mount Defiance, but he always believed that Ticonderoga was exposed and that Mount Independence on its own could withstand "a long and vigorous siege." St. Clair never shared that opinion, believing instead that each fort was necessary to support the other. Soon after the decision to retreat was made, he spoke with Udney Hay, deputy quartermaster general. As Hay recalled, St. Clair admitted that he did not have authorization from Schuyler to retreat, but told Hay, "If he remained there [at the forts], he would save his character and lose the army; if he went off, he would save the army and lose his character; the last of which he was determined to sacrifice to the cause."

St. Clair ordered Hay and other key officers to commence preparations for the withdrawal immediately, but the garrison was not to be informed until the last possible moment. Hay ordered his men to row their bateaux against a powerful north wind to bring away stores from Ticondergoa, but vast quantities of provisions, gear, and munitions were stranded. Men who had been sent to carry medical supplies worked "industriously" in the early evening, but once they learned of the retreat, many deserted.

The last American cannon on the Ticonderoga side were disabled by driving spikes into the touch holes, but the gunners did not use sledgehammers to knock off the trunnions or pivots for fear the sound would alert the enemy. Late in the afternoon and into the night, quartermasters issued each man extra cartridges plus five days of provisions, ostensibly to prepare them for action with the enemy, but the men were not to be told of the retreat. Pickets were sent out of the lines to make certain that British scouting parties did not come close enough to discover the Americans' intentions, and to intercept anyone attempting to desert and reveal the planned retreat to the enemy. A select rearguard of 450 men under the command of Ebenezer Francis was ordered to sweep "every thing off the ground upon the Ticonderoga side, to bring every man and beast" as they brought up the rear of the retreating army.

After midnight, officers roused their men and ordered them to pack baggage, strike tents, and prepare to march. From Ticonderoga, more than 2,000 men crossed the quarter-mile-long bobbing float bridge to Mount Independence. The 18-pounders in the Jersey

In the dark, British troops cross the floating bridge in pursuit of the retreating Americans. Greg Harlin for Smithsonian Magazine *Collection of the Mount Independence State Historic Site*

Redoubt by the lakeshore fired every seven minutes to distract the enemy and to cover the sounds of the retreat. The last soldiers to cross the lake removed planks from the floating logs to delay any British pursuit.

The retreating army was to take two routes south. Most of the soldiers would march southeast toward Rutland along the military road, while a select number of men, together with the women, the sick and their doctors, would travel south on the lake via boat to Skenesborough with as much equipment and supplies as they could carry.

The order to retreat shocked and surprised most of the men. Moses Greenleaf, now part of the rearguard, thought it the most "disagreeable News." Reverend Thomas Allen of Pittsfield, Massachusetts, who was there to fight as much as to preach, was outraged. The men were "in good spirits, enlivened with the prospect of action and eager for the battle," he wrote in the *Connecticut Courant*. Sick men reported for duty, saying, "We feel well enough to stand one warm battle." Patrick Cogan, a quartermaster for a New Hampshire regiment, wrote: "Such a Retreat was never heard of since the Creation of the world."

The scene on Mount Independence was chaotic. Brigadier General Roche de Fermoy, the highest-ranking officer on the Mount, was expected to direct the movement and loading of the supplies, cannon, and baggage at the south wharf, but after issuing orders he retired for the evening. When he was awakened around 2 a.m., Fermoy unaccountably put a torch to his cabin, "against positive orders" from St. Clair. The

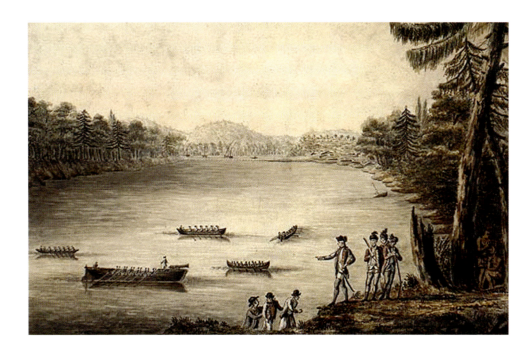

resulting bonfire illuminated the Mount. General Poor later recalled that from the Ticonderoga side he could clearly see the men taking down their tents, packing their baggage, and assembling to retreat. Fearing a British advance, Poor called in the pickets on the Ticonderoga side a half-hour early. Fortunately for St. Clair's plans, the British assumed the fire was a ruse to trick them into hastily advancing into cannon range, and they held back.

The flames heightened the disorder among the Americans. As the army began its march from Mount Independence, the militia panicked and rushed forward, drawing many Continental troops after them into a congested mass along the narrow, recently built military road to Rutland. St. Clair rode up and down

Opposite page: In 1777 Lieutenant James Hunter of the Royal Artillery painted this watercolor of Mount Independence (center) and Ticonderoga as seen by British gunboats and bateaux from the middle of Lake Champlain.
James Hunter / British Library

Above: In another painting based on firsthand observation, Lieutenant James Hunter depicted the American forts from a point on the western shore of Lake Champlain.
James Hunter / Archives Canada

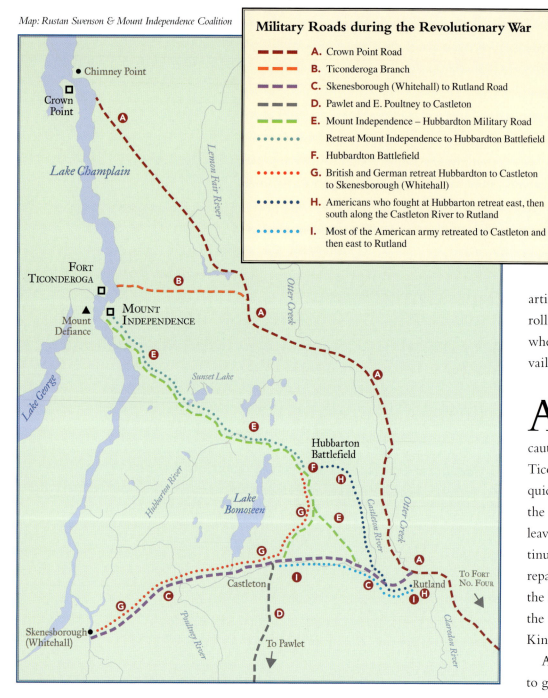

Map: Rustan Swenson & Mount Independence Coalition

the column, trying with little success to bring order to his disintegrating army. On the other hand, Francis's handpicked rearguard made an orderly withdrawal, taking up their position at the rear of the army.

At the southern wharf, women, children, and the sickest soldiers were embarked for the journey by water to Skenesborough. There, Udney Hay attempted to direct the loading of supplies, but he found that neither threats nor promises did much good. The high wind added to the chaos. Baldwin worked to get artificer tools aboard the bateaux, and then oversaw rolling a hundred barrels of gunpowder to the dock, where the men were "very cross, and hard to be prevailed with to do their duty."

Around 3 a.m., two deserters told General Fraser that the American army was retreating. After cautiously investigating for himself and finding the Ticonderoga fortifications abandoned, Fraser moved quickly to seize the ground. He ordered the colors of the 9th Regiment raised above the French Lines, and, leaving men to guard "a great quantity" of supplies, continued on. The partially damaged bridge was quickly repaired with new planks, and Fraser's brigade crossed the lake to Mount Independence, rushing up the hill to the Star Fort, where they raised the Union Jack—the King's Colors. By then dawn was brightening the sky.

As the sun rose, Baldwin was desperately pleading to get his personal baggage loaded onto one of the few

70 STRONG GROUND

remaining bateaux at the south landing. He eventually succeeded, after promising a barrel of rum to a captain, but by then British soldiers had reached the fortifications at the southern end of the Mount and fired down at the wharf. Baldwin and an artillery captain mounted and rode after the army, gathering up several drunken soldiers along the way and herding them forward.

There were several accounts of drunkenness among the retreating Americans. In one published in London a dozen years later, the British found four American gunners left to guard the bridge, "dead drunk by a cask of Madeira." The incident, although likely fictitious, appears in many histories and has become a signature detail of the retreat. In a more credible journal, Lieutenant William Digby of the 53rd Regiment marveled that the Americans had not aimed a cannon loaded with grapeshot at the bridge. He owed his life to the omission, he believed: "They would, in all probability, have destroyed all or most of us on the Boom."

At the Star Fort, Fraser's men began to plunder the wealth of supplies and personal possessions in the storehouses and barracks. A German surgeon, Julius Friedrich Wasmus, who followed later, found it to be "beyond description how much the enemy has left behind in ammunition, provisions, and such victuals as wine, rum, sugar, coffee, chocolate, butter, cheese, etc." Fraser noted with disgust at his men's lack of discipline: "It was with very great Difficulty I could prevent horrid irregularities." Finally by 5 a.m., order was restored, and Fraser ordered his men to pursue the main body of retreating Americans on the road to Rutland. "I was resolved to attack any body of rebels that I could come up with," he wrote. He sent a request to Burgoyne for support, "British if possible," meaning no Germans, whom he considered unreliable. Without having had time to bring provisions with them, a detachment of light infantry and grenadiers plus two companies of the 24th Regiment of Foot set out on the military road in pursuit.

Meanwhile, American vessels and heavily loaded bateaux sailed and rowed south on a part of Lake Champlain that is as narrow as a river as it threads its way through marshland to Skenesborough. It was a pleasant morning; the men and women on board the boats had made their escape; and the boom and barrier bridge would slow any pursuit, they assumed. Surgeon James Thacher remembered, "The drum and fife afforded us a favorite music; among the hospital stores we found many dozen of choice wine, and, breaking off their necks, we cheered our hearts with the nectareous contents."

With no one left to oppose his advance, Burgoyne ordered his gunboats forward against the lake obstructions between Ticonderoga and Mount Independence, "and the boom and one of the intermediate floats were

Above: A map of the Mount Independence and Ticonderoga area drawn by Thaddeus Kosciuszko for the court-martial of General St. Clair.

Opposite page: The main body of the American army retreated on the Hubbardton Military Road to Castleton, planning to join the remainder of the army in Skenesborough. Instead, following the Battle of Hubbardton, they marched east to Rutland.

A CONTROVERSIAL RETREAT 71

Above: American soldiers defend Monument Hill. Roy F. Heinrich, 1938 / © National Life Group. Used with permission. Below: The view from the Hubbardton Battlefield is largely unchanged from July 1777, especially during the annual weekend in which reenactors gather at the Vermont State Historic Site.

cut with great dexterity and dispatch." By eight o'clock, gunboats and the *Royal George* and *Inflexible* were passing the cliffs of the Mount. In the late afternoon, they caught up to the American flotilla crowding into Skenesborough. After a lopsided artillery duel that lasted a half-hour, the Americans burned and blew up what they could and fled on foot toward Fort Ann.

At the same time, nearly 4,000 Americans, pursued by 1,000 British and German troops, were strung out on the narrow military road leading 25 miles from Mount Independence to Castleton. The day had been exceedingly hot and humid; the terrain over which the Americans marched was alternately hilly and muddy, and mosquitoes were ever-present. They were burdened with supplies and pursued by a determined enemy—and most men had only had an hour or two of sleep. Some gave up and were taken prisoner. One of these "rebel" prisoners told Fraser that "Colonel Francis commanded the rear guard, and that he would be glad to surrender to the King's troops, rather than fall in to the hands of the Savages." Fraser later recalled "my men being fatigued I sent this person forward" with a demand that the Americans surrender. Francis sent word back to Fraser that he "disdain'd his proposal."

As the main body of the disorganized American army reassembled at Hubbardton in the late afternoon on July 6, St. Clair ordered Colonel Seth Warner—his senior and most experienced colonel—to take command of the rear guard when it arrived, and then to follow the main body to Castleton. Finding that the

A granite marker, erected by the Hands Cove Chapter of the DAR in 1933, commemorates the military road from Mount Independence to Hubbardton. Steve Zeoli photo

Previous page: A map of the Battle of Hubbardton drawn by Captain Johann Gerlach soon after the battle. The Americans hold the high ground—present-day Monument Hill—before retreating over Pittsford Ridge. The British and Germans claimed victory, but suffered so many casualties that they were unable to continue their pursuit. United States Military Academy

stragglers with the rear guard were totally exhausted, Warner chose to remain in Hubbardton for the night, but early on the morning of July 7, Fraser attacked. His men swept through the sickly American stragglers before they had roused themselves to continue their march, but when the British advance guard reached the hilltop known today as Monument Hill, they met disciplined Continental troops. The battle hung in the balance until the arrival of General Riedesel's Germans, sent by Burgoyne in support of Fraser. As the American line crumbled, Francis was killed, and Warner ordered a retreat over Pittsford Ridge.

By eighteenth-century standards, Hubbardton was an American defeat. The British and Germans held the ground and took 230 prisoners. But the victory was so costly that Fraser gave up any thought of pursuit. His men had suffered 70 killed, including Major Robert Grant of the 24th Regiment, and nearly 150 wounded, compared to American casualties of 40 dead and 100 wounded. Lieutenant James Hadden of the Royal Artillery, who heard accounts of the battle from fellow officers, wrote, "[Fraser's corps] certainly discover'd that neither they were invincible, nor the Rebels all Poltroons; On the contrary many of them acknowledged the Enemy behaved well, and look'd upon General Riedesel's fortunate arrival as a matter absolutely necessary."

After the battle, the American army regrouped in Rutland and marched south along Otter Creek. For a few days, their location was a mystery to General Schuyler, who wrote, "I am totally at a loss to conceive what has become of them." Congressman Samuel Adams, hoping to replace Schuyler with Gates, was blunter: "There is something droll enough in a General not knowing where to find the main Body of his Army."

In Manchester, Warner's men turned north to defend the Vermont frontier, while the remainder of St. Clair's army followed the Battenkill River west to the Hudson River, where once again they stood between Burgoyne and Albany.

News of the retreat shocked the American side: "The evacuation of Ticonderoga and Mount Independence is an event of chagrin and surprise not apprehended nor within the compass of my reasoning," Washington wrote to Schuyler. Samuel Adams commented, "It appears to me difficult to account for the Evacuation of those Posts even upon the Principle of Cowardice. The whole Conduct seems to carry evident Marks of Deliberation & Design." And in an absurd rumor, Burgoyne was said to have fired silver balls into Fort Ticonderoga to bribe St. Clair and Schuyler.

Congress recalled St. Clair and ordered Schuyler to be replaced by Horatio Gates. Both St. Clair and Schuyler were court-martialed: St. Clair for neglect of duty, cowardice, and treachery; Schuyler for not being present at the forts during the crisis. They were tried in the late summer of 1778, long after the defeats of July 1777 had been followed by the resounding victories at Bennington and Saratoga. By then it was widely recognized that the controversial retreat had saved the army, leading to Burgoyne's eventual surrender. Both men were exonerated with the highest honor.

Acquitted with the Highest Honour

A court-martial to try Arthur St. Clair for evacuating Ticonderoga and Mount Independence convened in August 1778 in White Plains, New York. St. Clair was charged with neglect of duty, cowardice, treachery, "inattention to the progress of the enemy," and "shamefully abandoning the posts."

Perceptions had changed since the night of July 5-6, 1777. Jeduthan Baldwin summed up the new mood in a letter to St. Clair written October 17, 1777, the day of Burgoyne's surrender at Saratoga. He congratulated his former commander on the victory. "The people in general have altered their sentiments with respect to the evacuation of Ticonderoga. The officers, and all who I now hear speak about it, say a better plan could not have been adopted, and nothing but leaving that place could have given us the success," he wrote.

St. Clair's indictment was brought by the Continental Congress at a time when relations between civilian and military authorities were strained, and the prosecution was unable to find Continental officers to serve as witnesses. Thaddeus Kosciuszko, Udney Hay, Enoch Poor, Jeduthan Baldwin, and Philip Schuyler all gave sympathetic testimony. Schuyler might have charged St. Clair with disobeying orders in leaving Mount Independence, but he did not. Evidence that St. Clair had undercounted the number of men in his command and the amount of provisions had no impact. St. Clair argued that he had foreseen that a retreat would draw Burgoyne into the country until "it would be difficult for him either to advance or retreat." The panel of officers, presided over by Major General Benjamin Lincoln, found St. Clair not guilty on all counts, "with the highest honour."

Schuyler was charged with being absent from Lake Champlain at the time of crisis. In his trial, he presented his voluminous personal papers to prove that as commander of the Northern Department, he had many responsibilities beyond the forts and was a master of the details. He too was acquitted with the highest honor. Although his military career was over, Schuyler served in the Continental Congress, the New York State Senate, and the U.S. Senate.

After his acquittal, St. Clair continued to have Washington's respect, but was given no battlefield commands. He was the next-to-the-last president of the increasingly weak Continental Congress and then governor of the Northwest Territory. In 1791, he led an army of a thousand men against a confederation of Indians under Little Turtle and Blue Jacket. Near the headwaters of the Wabash River, in present-day Ohio, St. Clair's force was destroyed. About 630 soldiers were killed and 280 wounded. Some 200 camp followers were also slain. Although largely forgotten today, St. Clair's Defeat, as the battle is sometimes called, was a far greater loss than Custer suffered at the Little Big Horn. St. Clair demanded a court-martial to clear his name, but President Washington was ready to move on. Anthony Wayne took command and in 1794 won the decisive Battle of Fallen Timbers.

Arthur St. Clair. Facsimile of a drawing by John Trumbull / Library of Congress

"On reception of this, you will at once surrender the Garrisons of Ticonderoga & mt. Independence, as it will very soon [be] out of your power to stop the Mighty Army of the Continent surrounding you on every side." — John Brown to H. Watson Powell, Sept. 18, 1777

CHAPTER EIGHT

A British and German Post Under Siege

"Our expectations were much surpassed… when we found in the morning of July 6th, that the rebels had left their fort quietly during the night," wrote August Wilhelm Du Roi, lieutenant and adjutant in the Prinz Friedrich Regiment. "We disembarked and marched with the band playing to Fort Ticonderoga. The colors of the enemy were hauled down at once, and the colors of the regiment hoisted on one of the bastions."

The hill opposite Ticonderoga, Du Roi wrote, "had been cleared of the wood, and a wooden fort been erected there, strengthening the whole with trenches and batteries. They had called this mountain on account of its location and their own intentions 'Mount Independence.' The whole was well done and showed no lack of clever engineers among the rebels."

Du Roi described the Great Bridge as "a piece of work which… does honor to human mind and power. It is only to be regretted that the work was commenced for fighting purposes. It therefore, will hardly be completed as it deserves." He compared it to "the work of Colossus in the fables of the heathen," one of the Seven Ancient Wonders of the World. And then notably for a man from a German duchy hired by a monarchy to suppress a young republic, he commented on the continuous work and "unfailing courage" of the men who nearly completed the bridge. "Such perseverance is seldom found in history, except in a republic, where a general participation in a common cause would inspire and hold it. It is rarely, if ever, found in monarchies."

At first Burgoyne assigned the 625 men of the Prinz Friedrich Regiment to Ticonderoga and the 62nd Regiment of Foot to Mount Independence, but by the end of July, the Germans took charge of the southern and most vulnerable portion of the Mount.

Brigadier General James Inglis Hamilton, now in command of the posts, faced the same challenges as St. Clair, but with only 900 men. As most of Burgoyne's army moved south to Skenesborough, Hamilton was left to defend an arc of fortifications, bridges, roads, and outposts that stretched five miles from the southern end of Mount Independence to Lake George Landing.

Militia from Massachusetts and Vermont supported by a contingent from Seth Warner's Continental regiment approach Mount Independence from the southeast. The Prinz Friedrich Regiment is well fortified on the southeastern heights, with British and Loyalist troops rushing to their support. Gary Zaboly / Mount Independence Coalition

The wounded make their way back from Hubbardton to the hospital on Mount Independence.
Ellen Viereck in
Independence Must Be Won
Collection of
Mount Independence
Historic Site

At the southern end of the Mount, the batteries begun by Kosciuszko and Baldwin were manned and strengthened. Work began on three additional blockhouses. The forest was cleared further away from the foot of the hill so that an attacker would be exposed to cannon fire before reaching the steep slope. The schooners *Maria* and *Carleton* anchored off the southern point of the Mount, where their guns could rake the neck of land with grapeshot. Four gunboats guarded the outlet of East Creek to the north of the floating bridge, which again served as a barrier. On the west side, a detachment defended old Fort Ticonderoga, while other men were stationed at a blockhouse at the falls of the La Chute River, Lake George Landing, and atop Mount Defiance.

In mid-August, Hamilton and the 62nd Regiment moved to Fort George and then rejoined Burgoyne along the Hudson, while Brigadier General H. Watson Powell took command on Lake Champlain, bringing with him the 53rd Regiment.

The lives of the Germans and British at the forts were not far different from those of the Americans. Men hoped for fresh provisions and were frequently disappointed. They burned abatis for firewood, provoking orders to cease. They drank when they could, and Hamilton struggled to control sutlers. On July 16, drunken British and German soldiers fought (much as men from Pennsylvania and Connecticut had six months earlier), and the garrison was reminded of the importance of "the harmony, which has hitherto so happily reigned between the two Nations." Finally, the sale of "spirituous liquors" was banned on Mount Independence. The inspector of hospitals called for two women from each regiment to serve as nurses. By fall, disease was taking a toll.

On July 27, a detachment of 60 British and 140 Germans, all under command of Major Friedrich von Hille, gathered at 5 a.m. on Mount Independence to bring the last wounded men back from Hubbardton. The party returned late on July 30. Many wounded men rode or staggered along, but 31 stretchers were each carried on the shoulders of four men. It was "a far sadder sight as they passed by than the 5th act of the tragedy of Julio and Romeo," wrote von Hille's son, Julius.

South of the twin forts, Burgoyne's army was creeping along, aimed at Albany. Short on supplies and horses for his cavalry, Burgoyne ordered a German regiment under command of Lieutenant Colonel Friedrich Baum to march to the east and raid the Continental supply depot in Bennington. On August 16, 1777, Baum ran straight into a combined force of New Hampshire militia under command of John Stark and militia from Vermont and Berkshire County, Massachusetts. The two armies met along the Walloomsack River in New York, ten miles from Bennington. Outnumbered by

American militiamen, Baum's Braunschweigers and Loyalists were slain or rounded up. Seth Warner's Continental regiment, which had been scouting in the north, reached the field in time to rout German reinforcements who might have swept through the celebrating militiamen.

The Battle of Bennington began a rapid change in fortune for the invading British. General Burgoyne wrote in despair to Lord George Germain, secretary of state for America: "The New Hampshire Grants [an early name for Vermont] in particular, a country unpeopled and almost unknown in the last war, now abounds in the most active and rebellious race on the continent and hangs like a gathering storm on my left."

Meanwhile, Horatio Gates, now commander of the Northern Department, together with General Benjamin Lincoln, devised another surprise move to the north. Parties of 500 men each were ordered to move against Skenesborough, Mount Independence, and Ticonderoga. Lincoln put militia Brigadier General Jonathan Warner in overall charge of the attacks, but the initiative was left to Colonel John Brown, a 32-year-old attorney from Pittsfield, Massachusetts, who knew the geography and had proved himself in Canada earlier in the war. (He would perish two years later in another New York skirmish.)

Brown's party of 500 men crossed narrow Lake Champlain at present-day Dresden, New York, and came into sight of the forts by the evening of September 17. Another party under Colonel Samuel Johnson approached Mount Independence through the thick forest on the neck of land between East Creek and the lake.

To coordinate the forces, Brown found two men willing to swim the lake with a message. As Richard Wallace, a Vermont ranger, recalled in his pension application 55 years later, he and Samuel Webster drank ginger and water before entering the cold lake. They were so near the *Maria* and the *Carleton* that they heard men talking on the deck. "The water was so chilling I thought I could never reach the opposite shore." Once Webster cried out, "For God's sake, Wallace, help me, for I am adrowning." But they both made the swim, and on the east side found an American sentry. After delivering their message, still cold and wet, they slept under borrowed blankets. "When we awoke in the

Richard Wallace and Samuel Webster swim Lake Champlain with a message from John Brown to Brigadier General Jonathan Warner, who was attacking Mount Independence.
Roy F. Heinrich, 1939 /
© National Life Group.
Printed with permission

Hessians and Brunswickers, Americans and Canadians

The Declaration of Independence presented a list of 27 grievances, "a history of repeated injuries and usurpations" perpetrated by King George III. "He is at this time transporting large Armies of foreign Mercenaries to compleat the works of death, desolation and tyranny already begun with circumstances of Cruelty and perfidy scarcely paralleled in the most barbarous ages, and totally unworthy the Head of a civilized nation," the delegates to the Continental Congress declared.

To Americans, all Germans who fought against them were Hessians. Germany in the eighteenth century was not a unified nation, but rather a jigsaw puzzle of 300 principalities, electorates, duchies, free cities, and feudal domains, many of which were nearly bankrupt. Renting armies to fight in foreign wars was a source of money. The largest force, about 17,000 men, came from Hesse-Cassel, hence the generic term Hessians.

Although Burgoyne's army included a regiment and an artillery company from Hesse-Hanau, most of the Germans, about 4,300, were from the principality of Braunschweig (Brunswick in English) in north central Germany, about a hundred miles south of Hamburg. The son of Duke Charles I of Braunschweig was married to George III's sister.

A German Dragoon. Staatsarchiv Wolfenbüttel

The commander of the German troops in the north was Friedrich Adolf Riedesel, Freiherr zu Eisenbach (1738-1800), a Hessian by birth. Major General Riedesel's nineteenth-century German biographer found him to be "impulsive and sensitive, vehement and passionate, and easily inclined to anger when his indignation was aroused." He was proud of the role of his men and ready to take offense if it was questioned.

Riedesel was also a loving husband and father. "Never have I suffered more than upon my departure this morning," he wrote his wife Frederika Charlotte upon leaving for America. "My heart was broken; and could I have gone back who knows what I might have done. But, my darling, God has placed me in my present calling, and I must follow it. . . . Guard most preciously the dear ones. I love them most fondly." With their daughters, she followed him to Canada and accompanied him through Burgoyne's campaign, captivity as a prisoner of war in the so-

Major General Friedrich Adolf Riedesel, Freiherr zu Eisenbach in the mid-1790s. He was 39 in the summer of 1777.
Johann Heinrich Schröder / National Museum, Warsaw

called Convention Army, and then postings in New York and Canada. They named a daughter born in 1780, Amerika.

Many Braunschweigers slipped away and became Americans as the Convention Army was marched from New England through the rich Pennsylvania-German countryside to Virginia and then back to Pennsylvania. At the war's end, thousands of Germans chose to stay in the United States and Canada.

morning all our troops destined for this service on both sides of the lake were in motion."

Overnight Brown's men climbed across the ridge that separates lakes George and Champlain, frequently hearing "the jingly of rattle snakes." They rushed out of the early morning fog to capture 293 British troops and Canadian workers, freeing 118 American prisoners of war in the process. At the same time, Vermont ranger captain Ebenezer Allen climbed Mount Defiance. He led the assault on the unfinished blockhouse, and as he told the story, "his men came after him like a stream of hornets to the charge."

They captured 21 prisoners, a 12-pounder, and two 6-pounders, along with powder and shot.

On the western side of the lake, only the old fort, which was manned by about a hundred men, remained in British possession. Brown sent a spirited surrender note: "On reception of this, you will at once surrender the Garrisons of Ticonderoga & mt. Independence, as it will very soon [be] out of your power to stop the Mighty Army of the Continent surrounding you on every side." Powell replied from Mount Independence, which was the heart of the defense, "The Garrison intrusted to my charge I shall defend to the last."

Brown's men held the elevated ground at the French Lines, but could go no further. They had only a few captured cannon, limited powder and shot, and no trained gunners. The heavy cannon from the Citadel on Mount Independence, a mile and a quarter away, fired at them, but with little effect. Brown recognized quickly that he could not take the old fort "without too great loss of Men."

On the other side of the lake, the attack on Mount Independence, which began an hour before daylight, September 18, was a feint to distract from Brown's activities across the lake. "Our picquets, however, were awake, sounded the alarm and in less than thirty seconds the entire regiment stood under arms and occupied the line," recalled Lieutenant Ernst Schroeder of the Prinz Friedrich Regiment.

That day and in the days that followed, the Americans facing Mount Independence hesitated to leave the protection of the woods. Thomas Johnson, an

Soldier in the Prinz Friedrich Regiment.
Staatsarchiv Wolfenbüttel

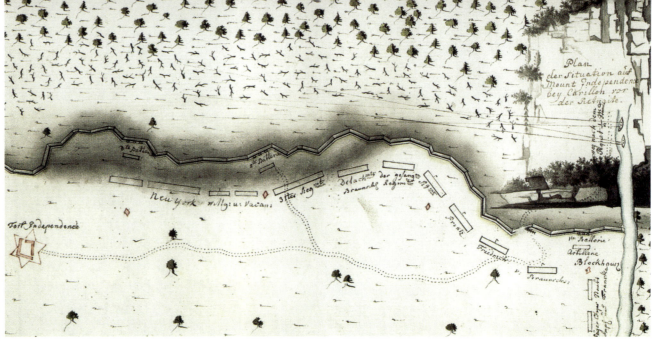

Right: Although not to scale, this German map gives a good depiction of the defenses at the southeast of Mount Independence. North is to the left. The narrow water is actually Lake Champlain. The positions of the Maria *and* Carleton *are accurate. Below: A German map showing all the defenses at Mount Independence and Ticonderoga in the fall of 1777.*
Staatsarchiv Marburg

innkeeper and merchant from Newbury, Vermont, on the upper Connecticut River, wrote to his wife Abigail, "The Grape Shot Ratel Like Hale Stones. But they Don't kill men. I Don't feel aney more Conscrnd Hear than I Did at home in my Busness." He fired his musket twice in three days and had trouble sleeping because of cannon fire.

In the fog or the dark, a few men crept into the no man's land between forest and hill and made off with plunder. General Warner sent his own surrender note, which was curtly refused in an answer delivered by Lieutenant Du Roi.

Atop Mount Independence, the Germans manned the southern two batteries and the lines stretching north. A contingent of the 53rd Regiment—described as a "very, very weak group" by Major von Hille—defended the northern battery. Having no idea how many Americans were hidden in the forest, the men on the Mount were on constant alert, waiting for the grand attack.

Lieutenant John Starke, captain of the *Maria*, summed up the siege of Mount Independence: "It is an undenyable truth that the Mount was never attacked by the Rebels otherwise than by Paper. The only living creature (except the paper messengers) who approached it after Sept. 18th was a poor strayed Cow, that in the night of the 21st being thick fog, caused a general Alarm."

Finally, in the rain on September 22, the men attacking Mount Independence slipped away on the military road, or boarded bateaux for Skenesborough. On captured vessels, Brown launched a raid against the British post on Diamond Island near the southern end of Lake George, but was driven off. He burned his boats and marched to Skenesborough, loaded with plunder.

General Powell attempted to put the best face on what had been a significant setback. The forts had held, and the men on Diamond Island had won a clear victory. "I must say I never saw Troops do their Duty with more alertness and cheerfulness," he told Guy Carleton. But the truth was far grimmer: the Lake Champlain forts were isolated and even the arrival of reinforcements made no difference. To the south, Burgoyne was on his own, facing disaster.

Jeduthan Baldwin had remained with the army that retreated from Mount Independence and was now part of the army that blocked Burgoyne's advance. On September 21, two days after the Battle of Freeman's Farm (also known as the First Battle of Saratoga), the news of the raid on the Lake Champlain forts reached the Americans at Saratoga. Thirteen cannon were fired, wrote Baldwin, and "a genl. Whooray throo all our camp." When Brown reached headquarters on October 1, Baldwin entered details of the victory in his journal: 315 prisoners taken; 110 prisoners of war freed; 200 bateaux, 17 gunboats, and one sloop destroyed; and £10,000 in plunder carried away.

On October 7, the two armies clashed again in a battle that has been called Bemis Heights or the Second Battle of Saratoga. Simon Fraser, who had taken Mount Independence three months earlier, was shot and died following a night of agony. Almost exactly a year after Valcour Island, Benedict Arnold led the

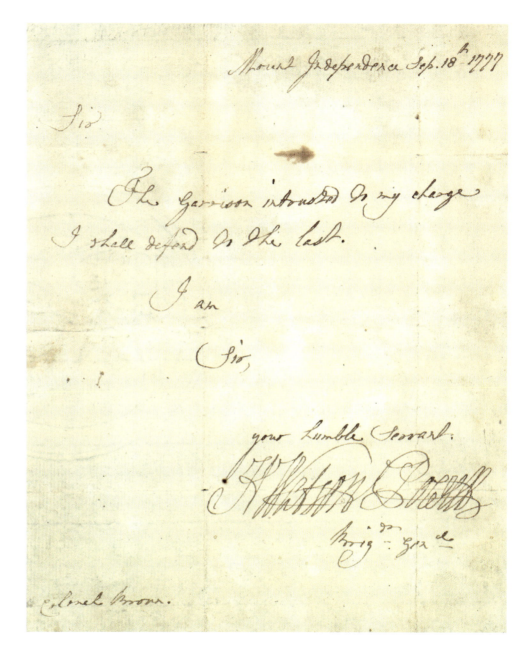

In the style of a gentleman, Brigadier General H. Watson Powell refused John Brown's call for the surrender of Mount Independence and Ticonderoga. Collection of J. Robert Maguire

A BRITISH AND GERMAN POST UNDER SIEGE

The Americans fortified the heights overlooking the Hudson River and blocked Burgoyne's advance. Two battles were fought on the ground that is now protected by the Saratoga National Historical Park. National Park Service

A statue of Seth Warner stands beneath the Bennington Battle Monument, which is a Vermont State Historic Site. The battle took place in New York, about ten miles away. The battlefield is a New York State Historic Site. Hunter Kahn photo

charge into the Breymann Redoubt and at the moment of victory was severely wounded in his left leg. Late on October 8 in a heavy rain, the British and Germans began a retreat to Saratoga, Philip Schuyler's village.

A sense of defeat hung upon the British and German forces at Mount Independence. On October 17, superstitious men watched the Union Jack in the Star Fort fall twice from its pole and believed they were seeing a bad omen. On the same day, just south of Schuyler's burned mansion, Burgoyne offered his sword to Horatio Gates in surrender.

At Mount Independence, General Powell knew that a reinvigorated American army would be returning, this time with enough artillery to succeed. He hoped Carleton would order a withdrawal, but the governor-general equivocated and in the end, like St. Clair, Powell called together his field officers to make the decision. They were unanimous that the posts could not be held.

Du Roi described the last moments of Mount Independence and Ticonderoga, November 8, 1777. "[B]efore daybreak, the signal was given to start the fires and to leave by blasting the last cannon. All at once we saw all the log houses, the store houses, the hospital, all the huts and cottages, everything which could be ruined by fire, in flames… The floating bridge was also cut down and burned." Fifty barrels of gunpowder erupted beneath Fort Ticonderoga and it "blew up high into the air."

When Major Benjamin Wait of the Vermont rangers took possession of Mount Independence, he found,

The campaign that began at Ticonderoga and Mount Independence ended when John Burgoyne surrendered to Horatio Gates in Saratoga (today's Schuylerville). John Trumbull commemorated the scene in 1821. His first version of the surrender is in the Rotunda of the U.S. Capitol; a later version is at Yale University. John Trumbull / Yale University Art Gallery

as Governor Thomas Chittenden reported to Gates, "Nothing of consequence there except several Boats which the Enemy had sank, in which there was some provisions; all Barracks, Houses, and Bridges were burnt. Cannon to the number of 40 were broke and spiked up."

In the fall of 1780, about a thousand British Regulars, Loyalists, and Indians came south on Lake Champlain. Passing Mount Independence in the dark, one bateau ran aground on a submerged pier of the Great Bridge, but the men were able to free themselves. The raiders seized Fort Ann and Fort George, and killed or captured most of Seth Warner's Regiment, who were the only remaining Continentals on the upper Hudson-Champlain corridor. They took captives and burned farms as far south as Ballston, 30 miles from Albany, before withdrawing.

On October 30, 1780, Lieutenant John Enys of the 29th Regiment spent much of the day on abandoned Mount Independence. In the late afternoon, his party set fire to brush and abatis. They rowed seven or eight miles south before learning that a truce had been agreed upon between British authorities and the leaders of Vermont, bringing that year's campaign to an end. As they made their way back north in the dark, the flames on Mount Independence "had very much the appearance of a Great Illumination."

EPILOGUE

Recognition and Preservation

"If we fail to tell our children these stories, if we don't bring them to places such as Mount Independence, we are doing them—and our country—a terrible disservice. We are depriving them of their heritage, and this country will be the poorer for it."

— RICHARD KETCHUM, DEDICATION OF THE MOUNT INDEPENDENCE VISITOR CENTER, JULY 27, 1996

On July 27, 1996, 3,000 people gathered at Mount Independence for the dedication of the Visitor Center and Museum. The event marked both a symbolic and a physical milestone along the road from obscurity to recognition for the historic site, which had been a footnote in the history books.

Mount Independence began to recede from memory soon after the British withdrawal. The features that made the Mount formidable in war were of no value in peacetime. Much of the "strong ground" is too rocky for cultivation, although a succession of determined farmers came and went, planting by the lake where Baldwin laid out the garrison's garden, grazing sheep and cattle, and tapping maples for sap to boil into syrup and sugar.

In 1785, the independent state of Vermont auctioned the "Cannon, Mortars, Mortar Beds, Bombshells, Carriage Wheels of Cast Iron in and about Mount Independence which...may be of service in making bar iron." Matthew Lyon, a founder of Fair Haven, won the bid for his iron works, 20 miles south. Lyon is best known as a hot-tempered, radical U.S. congressman. In 1798, he fought with Roger Griswold of Connecticut on the floor of the House of Represen-

The Mount Independence Visitor Center opened July 27, 1996, with thousands of people in attendance.
Collection of Mount Independence State Historic Site

SOUTH END OF LAKE CHAMPLAIN WITH RUINS OF FORT TICONDEROGA.

A view from Mount Independence in 1850.
New York Public Library

Writer and illustrator Benson Lossing (1813-1891) sketched Mount Independence's only gravestone in July 1848. Rain was threatening and he hurried his visit. He wrote, "The rude monument is a rough limestone, and the inscription 'M. Richardson Stoddard,' appeared as if carved with the point of a bayonet. The tenant was probably an officer of militia from a town formerly named Stoddard, in Vermont." The gravestone can still be seen. Although it is increasingly illegible, it appears to read, "N. RICHARDSON OF STADDARD ENG. DIED 1760". There is no Stoddard/Staddard in England or Vermont. Perhaps " Eng." refers to a company of engineers working on Fort Ticonderoga. The identity of the soldier is a mystery.

tatives and later that year was imprisoned under the Alien and Sedition Act for statements critical of President John Adams.

Illustrator and author Benson Lossing toured Mount Independence in the summer of 1848, researching his *Pictorial Field-Book of the American Revolution*. Lossing and his party landed near the site of the south wharf and walked up the steep hill to the plateau. Sugar maples, some of them 20 inches in diameter, had reclaimed the Mount, except for the parade grounds, which bore only "stinted vegetation." Remains of hundreds of houses were "scattered in all directions." The graves of "camp distemper" victims, he reported, "are thickly strewn among the trees."

Photo: Mount Independence State Historic Site

Lossing loved a good story. Just a few years earlier, he heard, money-diggers tried to uncover an "immense treasure," which they believed was left behind by the American army. They were scared off by boys with a lit jack o' lantern, and were now certain a "gentleman in black" guards the treasure and "sometimes takes an evening stroll on Mount Independence."

In the nineteenth century, Fort Ticonderoga—the ruin of the old fort that had been captured by Ethan Allen and served as barracks and headquarters in 1776-1777—became a tourist destination, owned by the Pell family. The importance of Mount Independence in the American Revolution was never entirely forgotten, but the details that would make events come alive were.

Mount Independence was an attractive spot for picnics; occasionally artists painted the view from the Mount. In 1908, the Hand's Cove chapter of the Daughters of the American Revolution dedicated a fourteen-foot

88 STRONG GROUND

granite obelisk as "a memorial to the brave soldiers buried here from 1775 to 1784 in unmarked graves and to the military importance of this mount in the War of the Revolution." In 1912, Sarah G. T. Pell purchased the northern 113 acres of Mount Independence. Today the nonprofit Fort Ticonderoga Association owns those acres. They are maintained by the Vermont historic site and are part of the site's extensive trail system.

In the years after World War II, a generation whose lives had been shaped by war realized that world-changing events had taken place in their own backyard. Joseph L. Wheeler, retired librarian at the Enoch Pratt Library in Baltimore and a nationally recognized authority on library administration, and his wife Mabel A. Wheeler began to research and map the military road that had been built in the fall of 1776 to connect the Mount to the Crown Point Road in Rutland. To understand the road, they needed to understand Mount Independence, which they called "the most interesting and important historic site in Vermont." Their detailed research first appeared in *Vermont History* in 1959 and was later reprinted as a book, *The Mount Independence-Hubbardton 1776 Military Road* (1968).

The Vermont Historic Sites Board and Graham Newell, a state senator from Caledonia County and chair of the Social Science Department at Lyndon State Teachers College, were instrumental in the 1961 purchase by the State of Vermont of the southern 103 acres.

The first survey of the Mount was conducted in 1966 and 1968 by three Middlebury College students—Chester Bowie, Erik Borg, and David Robinson—under the direction of Professor of History and Dean Thomas Reynolds and the newly formed Mount Independence Association. They marked nearly 150 sites of possible archaeological significance.

There were other steps on the way to recognition and preservation. Colonel John A. Williams, editor of the Vermont State Papers, wrote an introduction to Mount Independence for the April 1967 issue of *Vermont History*. He began his article with an unnamed member of the Vermont Historical Society who did not know the location of the Mount and ended with the assertion, "Mount Independence is worthy in every respect of preservation and appropriate development by

In 1873, John Howland Pell painted this scene of a picnic on Mount Independence.
Fort Ticonderoga Museum.

The Visitor Center, which recalls a beached bateau, was designed by the Burlington firm of Truex Cullins & Partners, winners of a design competition.

the people and the state of Vermont." After an official tour in 1968, David Kimball from the Office of Resource Planning of the National Park Service said Mount Independence was the most remarkably undisturbed and best preserved of all major Revolutionary War sites. In 1972, the Mount was awarded the status of National Historic Landmark.

Even as recognition of Mount Independence's importance grew, the site was threatened once again. The Vermont Electric Power Company (VELCO) developed a plan to construct two generating plants on a 2,200-acre site at Hough Crossing in the East Creek Valley. A 400-megawatt fossil-fueled power plant was to be followed in a few years by an 800-megawatt nuclear facility. Engineers envisioned a 500-foot smokestack and a dam on East Creek forming a 1,700-acre cooling pond.

J. Robert Maguire of Shoreham, an attorney and a member of the Mount Independence Association board of trustees, and John H. G. Pell, president of the Fort Ticonderoga Association, were leaders of the opposition. Maguire predicted what would happen if the plant were built. "In the end, as so often in the past, the country will suffer the ruin of a unique and irreplaceable historic landmark, one about which expert opinion is unanimous...that it represents a final opportunity to preserve a major Revolutionary site inviolate in the completely unspoiled setting. It would be difficult to conceive of a more reckless and wasteful misuse of a national resource; but it is more difficult not to despair of a society willing to accept such outrages in the name of 'growth' and 'progress.'"

Widespread opposition from the history and environmental communities forced VELCO to abandon the idea.

With the hiring in 1979 of John Dumville as its first

Above left: Archaeologists recognize Mount Independence as the least disturbed major Revolutionary War site. Mount Independence State Historic Site photo

Above right: Revolutionary War reenactors drill on Mount Independence.

historic sites operations chief, Vermont took a big step in protecting and promoting Mount Independence and other significant historic sites around the state. Dumville's undergraduate degree was from Lyndon, where he had studied with Professor Newell. He earned a master's degree from the University of Vermont in historic preservation and as a graduate student visited the Mount for picnics and camping. "It was a hayfield with cows grazing in it, but it was a fabulous untapped resource," he says.

Dumville, who retired at the end of 2014, oversaw the thoughtful evolution of the Mount from field to informative historic site. He says, "Mount Independence can be a challenging site to interpret. When people imagine a fort, they often think of a reconstructed fort. But at Mount Independence nothing was permanent. It was all earth and wood. It was a quick thing and then was abandoned and burned, and then reverted to woods, fields, and pasture."

He says, "I tell people, come to Mount Independence and let your mind work. You're not spoon-fed. The Mount makes you think."

In the summers of 1989, 1990, and 1992, David Starbuck, the preeminent archaeologist of military sites in the Upper Hudson–Lake Champlain corridor, led field schools, first under the auspices of the University of Vermont and then Castleton State College (now Castleton University).

Starbuck described his work on the Mount in *The Great Warpath: British Military Sites from Albany to Crown Point* (1999). He entitled one chapter, "The Most Intact Revolutionary War Site in America: Mount Independence." The Mount, he wrote, "is the largest military fortification in the North built specifically for the American Revolution.... I have never seen another military site, short of Masada in the State

RECOGNITION AND PRESERVATION 91

On a weekend in September, Revolutionary War reenactors camp on Mount Independence as part of the annual Soldiers Atop the Mount.

Right: Members of Mount Independence's Seth Warner Fife & Drum Corps march through the encampment.

of Israel, so well positioned to repel attackers."

In all, Starbuck's team discovered 30 cabins and houses, several barracks, a blockhouse, a storehouse, a dump, and a wealth of buttons, bottles, buckles, cups, and plates, examples of which are now on display in the museum.

Today a visitor to Mount Independence drives from Route 22A near the village of Orwell across the neck of land where the American army retreated in July 1777. It is now open farmland. The year 1880 appears in slate on the roof of a barn. Lake Champlain sparkles to the west. Wooded Mount Independence rises in front like the natural fortress it was. The sharp climb to the Visitor Center follows the road carved by soldiers.

Six miles of hiking trails wind through the forests, fields, and bedrock, taking visitors past most of the key military defenses. Among these trails is the Baldwin Interpretive Trail, which is suitable for outdoor wheelchairs. The 1.6-mile trail weaves through the sites of the Second and Third Brigade encampments, then passes the General Hospital, two blockhouses, and the Southern Battery. One stop is an overlook of Lake Champlain, Mount Defiance, and Fort Ticonderoga. In one sweeping view, a visitor sees why Mount Independence was both strategically important and physically imposing.

During his keynote address at the dedication of the Visitor Center in 1996, Pulitzer Prize-winning historian Richard Ketchum spoke about the men who had been stationed at Mount Independence 220 years before. Passing along these stories to future generations is necessary, Ketchum asserted. "If we fail to tell our children these stories," he said, "if we don't bring them to places such as Mount Independence, we are doing them—and our country—a terrible disservice. We are depriving them of their heritage, and this country will be the poorer for it."

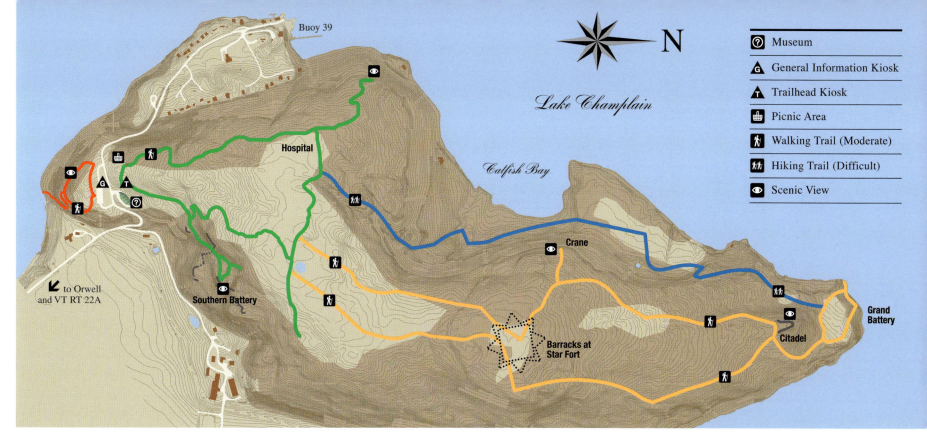

More than six miles of hiking trails lead visitors to the important sites on the Mount. The green Baldwin Interpretive Trail is suitable for outdoor wheelchairs. Mount Independence State Historic Site

In the museum, sculptures of soldiers talk about their experiences on the Mount.

A reenactor demonstrates a flintlock firearm.

Glossary of Military and 18th Century Terms

abatis (abbatis) – an entrenchment of felled trees with sharpened branches pointing toward the enemy to create a barrier; sometimes considered the barbed wire of the 18th century.

adjutant – a staff officer who transmits orders, details and assigns guards. The adjutant general is the principal staff officer of the army.

ague – a severe fever with chills and sweating that returns at regular intervals; perhaps malaria.

aide-de-camp – attendant of a general officer who receives and bears orders.

antiscorbutics – remedies that were thought to prevent scurvy, a disease caused by a lack of vitamin C in the diet; the science was only beginning to be understood in the 18th century.

artificer – a skilled mechanic or craftsman.

auxiliaries – foreign troops associated with those of a nation at war; historians sometimes use the term to refer to Germans fighting on the side of the British in the Revolutionary War.

bastions – a projecting part of a fortification; any strongly defended place or position.

battalion – military unit that can vary in size; often used interchangeably with regiment; the Pennsylvania regiments on Lake Champlain were referred to as battalions.

battery – an artillery unit of several cannon; a location where artillery is placed.

blockhouse – a fortification of logs and heavy timbers having loopholes from which to fire; typically two stories.

brigade – large military unit of two or more regiments, commanded by a brigadier general; on Mount Independence in 1776 there were three brigades usually commanded by a colonel.

brigadier – lowest rank of general; the Continental army in the Revolutionary War was led by major generals and brigadier generals.

breastworks – defensive military works, temporary or permanent, usually only about chest high.

carriage – a wheeled frame for carrying or holding a cannon.

cartridges – a casing of paper containing a charge of powder and shot for a musket or cannon.

colonel – commissioned officer one step below a brigadier general, often commanding a regiment.

Continental – the regular American army; or a soldier in the army paid or raised by the Continental Congress.

commissary – the person or persons in charge of stores or provisions.

daub – mud, plaster, or clay put on interwoven sticks (wattle) to form a solid wall.

deputy commissary general – assistant to the commissary-general.

detachment – part of a unit separated from its parent organization.

duchy – European territory ruled by a duke or duchess.

enfilade – gunfire that can rake lengthwise a line of troops; to fire at from the side where there is little defense.

engineer – soldier trained in constructing forts, bridges, and roads.

ensign – an officer ranking below a lieutenant.

fascines – bundles of sticks tied together and used in building earthworks for fortifications.

fatigue duty – physical labor, as the digging of ditches, cutting wood, building fortifications.

field officers – military leaders with the rank of major, lieutenant colonel, and colonel, who command on the "field of battle."

forage – searching for food and supplies; food suitable for horses and cattle.

French Lines – fortifications built in the French and Indian War northwest of Fort Ticonderoga by the French army; rebuilt by the Pennsylvania battalions in 1776 but still called the French Lines.

gondolas – flat–bottomed gunboats used on Lake Champlain as well as the St. Lawrence, Delaware and Hudson rivers.

howitzer – a cannon with a shorter barrel, firing at a higher angle than a cannon but less than a mortar.

lieutenant colonel – military leader between the rank of major and colonel; sometimes leader of a battalion.

light infantry – foot soldiers able to move quickly because they carried less equipment than regular troops, good for scouting; small, agile men.

log boom – a floating barrier of connected logs used to stop the advance of sailing ships.

major general – a high ranking officer, one step above a brigadier general; in the Continental Army major general was the highest rank.

mercenaries – soldiers hired by a foreign government to fight for pay; in the Revolutionary War Germans fighting on the side of the British were considered to be mercenaries by the Americans, although the soldiers were ordered to America by their ruler.

militia – the men of a town or county who gathered together occasionally for training and served for emergency defense.

muster – to call together or assemble troops for military duty; muster rolls kept track of men's presence.

picquets (pickets) – soldier or detachment of soldiers posted to guard a camp or position.

portage – act of transporting canoes, boats, and goods overland from one body of water to another; the carrying place.

quartermaster – officer responsible for the distribution of food, clothing, fuel, and other supplies for the military.

radeau – simply constructed vessel used as a naval gun platform; a floating fort, a large armed raft.

ration – food for one person for one day.

redoubt – enclosed fortification, earthwork or simple fortification placed within the line of a permanent fortification or in the field away from the main fortifications.

regiment – military unit usually commanded by a colonel; ideally eight to ten companies of 40 to 50 men each, but usually fewer.

scurvy – disease caused by lack of vitamin C in the diet, characterized by swollen and bleeding gums, making a person unable to function.

sutler – a peddler who sells goods and food to the army.

32-pounder – a cannon that fires an iron ball weighing 32 pounds.

touch hole – the opening in the barrel of a cannon or firearm through which the powder was ignited.

trunnion – one of two opposite cylindrical studs on a cannon, forming an axis on which it is elevated or depressed.

Recommended Reading and Sources

Baldwin, Jeduthan; Thomas Williams Baldwin, ed. *The Revolutionary Journal of Col. Jeduthan Baldwin, 1775-1778*, Bangor, Maine, 1906.

Barbieri, Michael. "Mount Independence: 'The most intact Revolutionary War site in America,'" online at the Journal of the American Revolution, https://allthingsliberty.com/2016/05/mount-independence-the-most-intact-revolutionary-war-site-in-america/

Bellico, Russell P. *Sail and Steam in the Mountains: A Maritime and Military History of Lake George and Lake Champlain*. Fleischmanns, N.Y.: Purple Mountain Press, 1992.

Cubbison, Douglas R. *The American Northern Theater Army in 1776: The Ruin and Reconstruction of the Continental Force*. Jefferson, N.C.: McFarland & Co., 2010.

Force, Peter, ed, *American Archives*, 4th series, vol. 6; 5th series, vols. 1-3. Washington D.C., 1837-1853. *American Archives* is searchable online at Northern Illinois University libraries: http://amarch.lib.niu.edu/.

Ketchum, Richard. *Saratoga: Turning Point of America's Revolutionary War*. New York: Henry Holt and Company, 1997.

Krueger, John W. "Troop Life at the Champlain Valley Forts During the American Revolution," *The Bulletin of the Fort Ticonderoga Museum* 14 (Summer 1982), 158-183; (Fall 1983), 220-249; (Summer 1984), 277-309.

Roberts, Kenneth. *Rabble in Arms*. New York: Doubleday & Company, 1933, 1957; Camden, Me.: Downeast Books, 1996; available digitally. Classic novel of the war on Lake Champlain.

Viereck, Phillip; Ellen Viereck, illus. *Independence Must Be Won*. New York: The John Day Company, 1964. A novel for older children.

Wickman, Donald H. *Built with Spirit, Deserted in Darkness: The American Occupation of Mount Independence, 1776-1777*, Master of Arts Thesis, University of Vermont, 1993.

Wilkinson, James. *Memoirs of My Own Times*, 1. Philadelphia: Abraham Small, 1816.

Zeoli, Stephen. *Mount Independence: The Enduring Legacy of a Unique Historic Place*. Hubbardton, Vt., 2011.

Chapter One

Beebe, Lewis. "Journal of a Physician on the Expedition Against Canada, 1776," *The Pennsylvania Magazine of History and Biography* 59 (October 1935): 321-361.

Force, Peter, ed, *American Archives*, Series 4, vol. 6; Series 5, vol. 1. (see above)

Gerlach, Don R. *Proud Patriot: Philip Schuyler and the War of Independence, 1775-1783*. Syracuse, N.Y.: Syracuse University Press, 1987.

Trumbull, John, *Autobiography, Reminiscences and Letters of John Trumbull from 1756 to 1841*. New York: Wiley and Putnam, 1841.

Chapter Two

Baldwin, Jeduthan. *The Revolutionary Journal of Col. Jeduthan Baldwin, 1775-1778*, (see above).

Beal, Benjamin. *Benjamin Beal Journal*. American Antiquarian Society, Worcester, Mass.

Butterfield, Charles H., ed. *A Narrative of Soldiery: The Journal of Zephaniah Shepardson, Guilford, Vermont, 1826*. Charles H. Butterfield, 2000.

Calloway, Colin G. *The American Revolution in Indian Country*. New York: Cambridge University Press, 1995.

Force, Peter, ed, *American Archives*, Series 5, vol. 1-2. (see above)

Frazer, Persifor. *General Persifor Frazer: A Memoir Compiled Principally from his Own Papers*. Philadelphia, 1907.

Greenwood, John; Isaac J. Greenwood, ed. *The Revolutionary Services of John Greenwood of Boston and New York, 1775-1783*. New York, 1922.

Mintz, Max M. *The Generals of Saratoga: John Burgoyne & Horatio Gates*. New Haven: Yale University Press, 1990.

Nash, Gary; and Graham Russell Hodges. *Friends of Liberty: A Tale of Three Patriots, Two Revolutions, and the Betrayal that Divided a Nation: Thomas Jefferson, Thaddeus Kosciuszko, and Agrippa Hull*, New York: Basic Books, 2008.

Nelson, Paul David. *General Horatio Gates: A Biography*. Baton Rouge: Louisiana State University Press, 1976.

Quarles, Benjamin. *The Negro in the American Revolution*. Chapel Hill: Univeristy of North Carolina Press, 1961.

Robbins, Ammi. *Journal of the Rev. Ammi R. Robbins, A Chaplain in the American Army, in the Northern Campaign of 1776*. New Haven: B.L. Hamlen, 1850.

Saillant, John. *Black Puritan, Black Republican: The Life and Thought of Lemuel Haynes, 1753-1833*. New York, Oxford University Press, 2003.

Salsig, Doyen. *Parole: Quebec; Countersign: Ticonderoga: Second New Jersey Regimental Orderly Book 1776*. Rutherford, N.J.: Fairleigh Dickinson University Press, 1980.

Stillé, James. *Major-General Anthony Wayne and the Pennsylvania Line in the Continental Army*. Philadelphia: J.B. Lippincott Company, 1893.

Thacher, James. *A Military Journal During the American Revolutionary War from 1775 to 1783*. Boston: Cotton and Barnard, 1827.

"The Wayne Orderly Book," *Bulletin of the Fort Ticonderoga Museum* 11 (September 1963), 94-204.

Chapter Three

Baldwin, Jeduthan. *The Revolutionary Journal of Col. Jeduthan Baldwin, 1775-1778*, (see above)

Bratten, John R. *The Gondola Philadelphia & the Battle of Lake Champlain*. College Station: Texas A & M University Press, 2002.

Burton, Jonathan; Isaac W. Hammond, ed. *Diary and Orderly Book of Sergeant Jonathan Burton of Wilton, N.H.: While in Service in the Army on Winter Hill, Dec. 10, 1775-Jan. 26, 1776, and of the Same Soldier as Lieutenant Jonathan Burton, While in the Canada Expedition at Mount Independence, Aug. 1, 1776-Nov. 29, 1776*. Concord, N.H.: Republican Press Association, 1885.

Force, Peter, ed, *American Archives*, Series 5, vol. 1-2. (see above)

Martin, James Kirby. *Benedict Arnold, Revolutionary Hero: An American Warrior Reconsidered*. New York University Press, NY, 1997.

Morgan, Appleton, ed. "The Diary of Colonel Elisha Porter, of Hadley, Massachusetts," *The Magazine of American History* 30 (1893), 85-206.

Morgan, William James, ed. *Naval Documents of the American Revolution*, vols. 5-6 (Washington, D.C., 1970-1974). All 12 volumes are online at www.history.navy.mil/research/publications

Nelson, James L. *Benedict Arnold's Navy: The Ragtag Fleet that Lost the Battle of Lake Champlain but Won the American Revolution*. New York: McGraw Hill, 2006.

Orderly Book of the Northern Army, at Ticonderoga and Mt. Independence from October 17th, 1776, to January 8th, 1777, with Biographical and Explanatory Notes and an Appendix. Albany, N.Y.: J. Munsell, 1859.

Wells, Bayze. *Journal of Bayze Well of Farmington, May 1775-February 1777, At the Northward and Canada*, in *Collections of the Connecticut Historical Society* 7 (Hartford, 1899): 241-296.

Chapter Four

Beebe, Lewis. "Journal of a Physician on the Expedition Against Canada, 1776," (see above)

Chamberlain, William. "Letter of Gen. William Chamberlain, March 2, 1827," in *Proceedings of the Massachusetts Historical Society*, Series 2 (Boston, 1896), 10: 500.

Elmer, Ebenezer. "Journal of Ebenezer Elmer," *Proceedings of the New Jersey Historical Society* 3 (1848): 21-56; 90-102.

Greenwood, John. *The Revolutionary Services of John Greenwood* (see above).

Lacey, John. "Memoirs of Brigadier-General John Lacey of Pennsylvania," *The Pennsylvania Magazine of History and Biography* 25 (1901).

Mayer, Holly A. *Belonging to the Army: Camp Followers and Community during the American Revolution*. Columbia, S.C.: University of South Carolina Press, 1999.

Riedesel, Friederike [Frederika in many sources] Charlotte Luise Von. *Letters and Journal Relating to the War of the American Revolution and the Capture of the Germans Troops at Saratoga*. Albany, N.Y.: Joel Munsell, 1867.

Thacher, James. *A Military Journal*. (see above)

Wayne letters in Stillé, *Major-General Anthony Wayne*. (see above)

Wells, Bayze. *Journal of Bayze Well of Farmington, May 1775-February 1777*. (see above)

Chapter Five

Baldwin, Jeduthan. *The Revolutionary Journal of Col. Jeduthan Baldwin, 1775-1778.* (see above)

Haiman, Miecislaus. *Kosciuszko in the American Revolution.* New York: The Kosciuszko Foundation and the Polish Institute of Arts and Science, 1975; original, 1943.

The Journals of the Continental Congress and *The Letters of Delegates to Congress* can be found online at the Library of Congress, American Memory.

McLaughlin, Scott A. *History Told from the Depths of Lake Champlain: 1992-1993 Fort Ticonderoga-Mount Independence Submerged Cultural Resource Survey.* Master of Arts Dissertation, Texas A&M University, May 2000.

Stockton, Richard and George Clymer. "Report of the Committee sent to the Northern Department," *Orderly Book of the Northern Army, at Ticonderoga and Mt. Independence, (see above),* 162-174.

Storozynski, Alex. *The Peasant Prince: Thaddeus Kosciuszko and the Age of Revolution.* New York: Thomas Dunne Books, 2009.

Chapter Six

Baldwin, Jeduthan. *The Revolutionary Journal of Col. Jeduthan Baldwin, 1775-1778.* (see above)

McLaughlin, Scott A. *History Told from the Depths of Lake Champlain.* (see above)

Mintz, Max M. *The Generals of Saratoga: John Burgoyne & Horatio Gates.* (see above)

Smith, William Henry. *The St. Clair Papers: The Life and Public Services of Arthur St. Clair.* Cincinnati, Ohio: Robert Clarke, 1882.

"Trial of Major General St. Clair, August, 1778," *Collections of the New-York Historical Society for the Year 1880* 13 (New York, 1881): 1-171.

"The Trial of Major General Schuyler, October 1778," *Collections of the New-York Historical Society for the Year 1879* 12 (New York, 1880): 1-211.

Wilkinson, James. *Memoirs of My Own Times,* 1. Philadelphia: Abraham Small, 1816.

Chapter Seven

Baldwin, Jeduthan. *The Revolutionary Journal of Col. Jeduthan Baldwin, 1775-1778.* (see above)

Burgoyne, John. *A State of the Expedition from Canada as Laid Before the House of Commons by Lieutenant-General Burgoyne and Verified by Evidence; with a Collections of Authentic Documents.* London: J. Almon, 1780.

Calloway, Colin. *The Victory with No Name: The Native American Defeat of the First American Army.* Oxford University Press, 2015.

De Fonblanque, Edward. *Political and Military Episodes in the Latter Half of the Eighteenth Century Derived from the Life and Correspondence of the Right Hon. John Burgoyne, General, Statesman, Dramatist.* London: MacMillan and Co., 1876.

Doblin, Helga, trans. *An Eyewitness Account of the American Revolution and New England Life: The Journal of J. F. Wasmus, German Company Surgeon, 1776-1783.* New York: Greenwood Press, 1990.

Duling, Ennis. "Thomas Anburey at the Battle of Hubbardton: How a Fraudulent Source Misled Historians," *Vermont History* 78 (Winter/Spring, 2010): 1-14.

"Gen. Fraser's account of Burgoyne's campaign on Lake Champlain and the Battle of Hubbardton (Stevens' Facsimiles, vol. XVI, no. 1571) Therein entitled 'Brigadier General Simon Fraser to [John Robinson]. Abergavenney manuscripts at Eridge castle.' Endorsed 'Copy from Brig'r Fraser, 13th July, 1777, Skeensborough.'" *Proceedings of the Vermont Historical Society* 4 (1899): 139-147.

Kingsley, Ronald F., Harvey Alexander, and Eric Schnitzer, "German Auxiliary Project: The Incursion to Mount Independence, July 1777, Part II: The Advance Against Mount Independence," *The Hessians: Journal of the Johannes Schwalm Historical Association* 9 (2006): 53-73.

Letters of the Delegates to Congress (see above).

Lunt, James. *John Burgoyne of Saratoga.* New York: Harcourt Brace Jovanovich, 1975.

Mintz, Max M. *The Generals of Saratoga: John Burgoyne & Horatio Gates.* (see above)

Morgan, Ron R. "Arthur St. Clair's Decision to Abandon Fort Ticonderoga and Mount Independence," online at the Journal of the American Revolution: https://

allthingsliberty.com/2016/05/arthur-st-clairs-decision-to-abandon-fort-ticonderoga-and-mount-independence/

Morgan, Ron R. "'Shamefully abandoning the posts of Ticonderoga and Mount Independence, in his charge': The Court Martial of Major General Arthur St. Clair and the Verdict of History," online at the Mount Independence Coalition website.

Rogers, Horatio, ed. *Hadden's Journal and Orderly Books: A Journal Kept in Canada and Upon Burgoyne's Campaign in 1776 and 1777*. Albany, N.Y., J Munsell's Sons, 1884.

Smith, William Henry. *The St. Clair Papers*. (see above).

"The Trial of Major General Schuyler." (see above)

Venter, Bruce M. *The Battle of Hubbardton: The Rear Guard Action that Saved America*. Charleston, S.C.: The History Press, 2015.

Wickman, Donald H. "'Breakfast on Chocolate': The Diary of Moses Greenleaf, 1777," *Bulletin of the Fort Ticonderoga Museum* 15, no. 6 (1997): 483-506.

Williams, John. *The Battle of Hubbardton: The American Rebels Stem the Tide*. Vermont Division for Historic Preservation, 1988.

Chapter Eight

Clarke, William Butler. "Colonel John Brown's Expedition against Ticonderoga and Diamond Island, 1777," *The New England Historical and Genealogical Register* 74 (Oct. 1920): 284-293.

Collections of the Vermont Historical Society 1. Montpelier, Vt.: J. & J.M. Pollard, 1870-1871.

Dann, John C. *The Revolution Remembered: Eyewitness Accounts of the War for Independence*. Chicago: The University of Chicago Press, 1980.

Doblin, Helga, trans. *The American Revolution, Garrison Life in French Canada and New York: Journal of an Officer in the Prinz Friedrich Regiment, 1776-1783*. Westport, Conn.: Greenwood Press, 1993.

Du Roi, August Wilhelm; Charlotte S.J. Epping, ed. and trans. "Journal of Du Roi the Elder, Lieutenant and Adjutant, in the Service of the Duke of Brunswick 1776-1777," *German American Annals*, 10 (September-December, 1911), 40-64, 77-128, 131-239.

Enys, John; Elizabeth Cometti, ed. *The American Journals of Lt. John Enys*. Syracuse, N.Y.: Syracuse University Press, 1976.

Howe, Archibald M. "Colonel John Brown of Pittsfield, Massachusetts: The Brave Accuser of Benedict Arnold." Boston: W. B. Clarke Co., 1908.

Hoyt, Edward A. and Ronald F. Kingsley. "The Pawlet Expedition, September 1777," *Vermont History* 25 (Summer/Fall 2007): 69-100.

Pell, Robert T. "John Brown and the Dash for Ticonderoga," *Bulletin of the Fort Ticonderoga Museum* 2 (January 1930): 23-40.

Riedesel, Friederike. *Letters and Journal Relating to the War of the American Revolution and the Capture of the Germans Troops at Saratoga*. (see above).

Riedesel, Friedrich Adolf; Max von Eelking, ed,; William L. Stone, trans. *Memoirs and Letters and Journals of Major General Riedesel, During His Residence in American*. Albany, N.Y.: J. Munsell, 1868.

Roberts, Lemuel. *Memoirs of Captain Lemuel Roberts*. Bennington, Vt.: Anthony Haswell, 1809.

Van Schaack, Henry Cruger. "Colonel John Brown: A Prophet hath no honor in his own country." Ms. S-24, Massachusetts Historical Society, Boston.

Chapter Nine

Lossing, Benson. *The Pictorial Field-Book of the Revolution*. New York: Harper & Brothers, 1850-1851.

McLaughlin, Scott. *History Told from the Depths of Lake Champlain* (see above).

Starbuck, David R. *The Great Warpath: British Military Sites from Albany to Crown Point*. Hanover, N.H.: University Press of New England, 1999.

Wheeler, Joseph L., and Mabel A. Wheeler. *The Mount Independence-Hubbardton 1776 Military Road*. Benson, Vt., 1968.

Williams, John A. "Mount Independence in Time of War, 1776-1783," *Vermont History* 35 (April 1967) 2: 60-79

Index

Images and maps are indicated by italicized page numbers.

abatis, 23–24, 58, 61, 78
Abenaki, 15, *15*
Abercrombie, James, 18, 29
Acland, Harriet, 45
Acland, John Dyke, 45
Adams, Samuel, 32, 74
African American soldiers, 19, 21
ague, 24
alcohol, 30, 43, 71, 78
Alien and Sedition Act, 88
Allen, Ebenezer, 81
Allen, Ethan, 11
Allen, Thomas, 69
American troops, discord among, 9, 19
Amherst, Jeffrey, 11
Amsbury, William, 58
Anburey, Thomas, *59*
archaeology, 30, 89, *91*, 91–92. *see also* artifacts
Arnold, Benedict, *29*
    assumes command of navy, 31
    Battle of Valcour Island, 32, 36, *36*
    builds navy, 28
    captures Fort Ticonderoga, 11
    clash with Jacobus Wynkoop, 31
    commands First Brigade, 18
    decision to fortify Mount Independence, 12
    leaves for winter, 39
    siege of Québec, 7–8
    on strength of troops, 32
    wounded at Saratoga, 83–84
Arnold Bay, 36
artifacts. *see also* archaeology
    ax, *18*
    bar shot, *32*
    button, *20*
    cannon, *60*
    cooking pot, *30*
    creepers, *43*
    fireplace, *59*
    flintlock musket, *31*
    fork, *30*
    grenade, *32*
    medicine vial, *20*
    powder horn, *22, 42*
    wine bottle, *43*
artificers, 24
ax (artifact), *18*

bake house, 24
Baldwin, Jeduthan, 17–25
    on anticipated siege, 62
    Arthur St. Clair court-martial, 75
    background, 17
    on Brown's raid, 83
    on camp life, 54
    construction
        barracks, 40
        batteries, 61
        Citadel, 24
        crane, 52
        floating bridge, 33
        Grand Battery, 23–24
        Great Bridge, 50–52
        log boom, 33
    on construction, 16, 23
    craftsmen, 23
    on evacuation, 75
    explores Mount Independence, 17
    garden, 30, 52
    illness, 24–25
    on imminent British attack, 33
    Mount Hope, 24
    plans to strengthen forts, 48
    relationship with Kosciuszko, 54
    retreat, 70–71
Baldwin Interpretive Trail, 92, *93*
bar shot (artifact), *32*
Barber, Francis, 44
Barrett, John, 31
Baum, Friedrich, 78–79
Bedel, Timothy, 19
Bedel's New Hampshire Rangers, *16*, 17, 19, 22
Beebe, Lewis, 5–6, 20, 27, 33, 39
Bemis Heights, 83
Bennington, Battle Monument, *84*
Bennington, Battle of, 78–79
bilious fever, 22
Bitawbagok (Lake Between), 15
black soldiers. *see* African American soldiers
Bland, Humphrey, 18
Bond, William, 22
Borg, Erik, 89
Bouquet River, 61
Bowie, Chester, 89
Braunschweigers, 21, 79, 80
bridge. *see* floating bridge; Great Bridge
British army
    9th Regiment of Foot, 70
    24th Regiment of Foot, 71, 74
    29th Regiment of Foot, 85
    53rd Regiment of Foot, 71, 78, 82
    62nd Regiment of Foot, 77, 78
British fleet, 28–29. *see also* names of specific vessels
Brown, John, 76, 79 81-83
Browne, John, 60
Brunswickers, 21, 79, 80
Burgoyne, John, 63, *63*
    1777 campaign, *3*
    advances south, 58, 66, 71–72
    on Battle of Bennington, 79
    invasion, *56–57*
    size of force, 62
    surrenders, 84, *85*
    three-pronged attack, 63
Burrall, Charles, 5, 17, 22, 42
button (artifact), *20*

caissons, 48, *53*
Calfe, John, 22
camp distemper, 88
camp followers, 30, 45, *45*
Canada, invasion of, 5, *6*
cannon, 60, *60*, 84
    Citadel, 24
    disabled, 67
    Grand Battery, 24
    moved from Ticonderoga, 61
    naval, 31–32
Carleton (British schooner), 29, 78, 79, *82*
Carleton, Guy, *29*
    advance halted, 35
    Battle of Valcour Island, 32
    naval fleet, 28–29
    reconnoiters American defenses, 33–35
    takes Crown Point, 33
Castleton (Vermont), 70, 72

Catfish Bay, *14*, 52, *61*
Champlain, Samuel de, 15
chert, 15
chevaux-de-frise, 48
Chimney Point, 6, 61
Chittenden, Thomas, 85
Citadel, 24, *34, 35*, 48
Clymer, George, 40, 47
Cogan, Patrick, 69
Congress (American galley), 36
Connecticut Courant (newspaper), 69
Connecticut troops, 5, 17, 42
Connor, Samuel, 35
Continental Congress
    appoints Schuyler, 54
    approves new fortifications, 48
    declares independence, 19
    feuds with Schuyler, 48, 50
    on George III, 80
    orders to St. Clair, 58
    and rations, 30
    Schuyler court-martial, 74–75
    St. Clair court-martial, 75
    strengthens Mount Independence, 53
cooking pot (artifact), *30*
crane, 52, *61*
creepers (artifact), *43*
Crown Point
Crown Point Military Road, *7*, 31, *70*, 89
Crown Point-Chimney Point narrows, 6, 7

Daughters of the American Revolution, 44, 74, 88–89
Dayton, Elias, 40
deserters, 67, 70
Diamond Island, 83
diet. *see* soldiers, diet
Digby, William, 71
disease, 20, *20*, 22, 41, 43, 48. *see also* specific diseases
Down, Jacob, 21
Downs, David, 42
drunkenness. *see* alcohol
Du Roi, August Wilhelm, 77, 82, 84
Dumville, John, 90–91
Dunlap, James, 35
dysentery, 20, 63

East Creek, *4*, 15, *15*, 66, 78
East Point, 1, 18, 20
Elmer, Ebenezer, 40–41
    on cold, 39, 41, 43
    on discipline, 43
    leaves Mount Independence, 44
    on Margaret Hay, 45
    on winter disease/death, 44
Enys, John, 85
Erbprinz Regiment, 66
Essex (British ship), 60

fascines, 23
fatigue duty (parties), 23, 61, 62
Fermoy, Matthias Alexis Roche de, 58, 69
Ferris Bay, 36
fireplace (artifact), *59*
First Brigade, 18
flintlock musket (artifact), *31*
floating bridge, 67
    broken, 40
    constructed, 33
    destroyed by retreating British, 84
    disabled, 69
    repaired, 51, 52
    retreat over, 67, *67*
food. *see* soldiers, diet
fork (artifact), *30*
Fort Ann, 72, 85
Fort Carillon, 9, *18*. *see also* Fort Ticonderoga
Fort Crown Point, 7, *7*, 14, 27, 33
Fort George, 27, 47, 78, 85
Fort Number 4, 31
Fort Ticonderoga
    captured by Americans, 11
    decision to abandon, 59
    destroyed by retreating British, 84
    images
        Hunter, *68*
        from Mount Defiance, *64–65*
        view of from Citadel, *23*
    maps
        German, *82*
        Hudson/Champlain corridor, *7*
        Kosciuszko, *71*
        Michel Capitaine de Chesnoy, *viii*
        topographic, *14*
    named, 11
    in nineteenth century, 88
    plans to recapture, 79
    retreat from, 67, 69
    strengthened, 24
    supplies removed from, 59
Fort Ticonderoga Association, 89, 90
foundation (officer's house), 24
Fourth Brigade, 19
Francis, Ebenezer, 67, 70, 72, 74
Fraser, Alexander, 62
Fraser, Simon
    Battle of Hubbardton, 74
    captures Mount Hope, 62
    death, 83
    fortifies Mount Defiance, 65–66
    pursues retreating troops, 71
    requests surrender, 72
    takes Ticonderoga/Mount Independence, 70
Frazer, Persifor, 19, 21
Freeman's Farm, Battle of, 83
French and Indian War, 6–7, 9
French Lines, *18*, *29*, 34, 62, 70, 81

Gall, Wilhelm von, 66
garden, 30, *52*
Gates (American galley), 34–35, 43
Gates, Horatio, 25, *25*
    appointed commander, 50
    arming navy, 27–28
    assigns naval command to Arnold, 31
    attempts to stop British advance, 33
    background, 8
    Burgoyne surrenders to, 84, *85*
    and conflicts among troops, 19
    decision to fortify Mount Independence, 12
    encourages troops, 22–23, 25
    on fleet, 31–32
    leaves for winter, 39
    leaves Ticonderoga/Mount Independence, 54
    orders to Arnold, 36
    orders to Kosciuszko, 54
    plans to recapture forts, 79
    relationship with Schuyler, 9, 27, 48, 50, 53, 54
    replaces Schuyler, 74
    on supplies, 30, 32, 47–48
General Hospital, 47, 54, 92

George III, 80
Gerlach, Johann, *73*, 74
Germain, George, 79
German troops, 80, *80*
    African Americans, 21
    approach Mount Independence, 66
    Battle of Bennington, 78–79
    Battle of Hubbardton, 74
    Erbprinz Regiment, 66
    numbers, 45, 62
    Prinz Friedrich Regiment, 77, 81, *81*
    at surrender, 45
    tension with British troops, 78
    at Ticonderoga/Mount Independence, 77, 82
ghost story, 88
Gilder, Henry, 36
Gilliland's Creek, 61
Grand Battery, 23–24, *34*
Grant, Robert, 74
graves, 88–89
gravestone, 88, *88*
Great Bridge, *50*
    British praise for, 77
    construction, *46*, 50–52
    planned, 48
    repaired by British, 70
    timbers, 52
Greaton, John, 19, 22, 34
Greenleaf, Moses, 54, 66, 69
Greenwood, John, 17
grenade (artifact), *32*
Griswold, Roger, 87
guardhouses, 24

Hadden, James, 74
Hamilton, Alexander, 25
Hamilton, James Inglis, 77–78
Hancock, John, 50, 58
Hands Cove Chapter of the DAR, 44, 74, 88–89
Harlin, Greg, *20*, *41*, *56–57*, *64–65*, *67*
Hay, Margaret, 45
Hay, Udney
    preparation for retreat, 67
    retreat to Skenesborough, 70
    on St. Clair, 66–67
    St. Clair court-martial, 75
    on supplies, 53

wife, 45
Haynes, Lemuel, 21
Heinrich, Roy F., *28*, *72*, 79
Hessians, 80
hiking trails, 92, *93*
Hille, Friedrich Wilhelm von, 78, 82
Hille, Julius Friedrich von, 78
Horsehoe Battery, 34
hospitals
    Fort George, 27, 47
    Mount Independence, *20*, 24, 43, 61
    General Hospital, 47, 51, 54, 92
Hough Crossing, 90
Howe, William, 58, 63
Hubbardton, Battle of, 72–74, *73*
    African American soldiers at, 21
    casualties, 74, 78, *78*
    map, *70*
    prisoners, 74
Hudson River, 6, 63
Hudson-Champlain corridor, 6–7, 35, 85, 91
Hull, Agrippa, 21, *21*
Hunter, James, *68*, 69

Île-aux-Têtes, 36
illness. *see* disease
independence declared, 19
Independence Must Be Won (Viereck), *61*, *78*
Indians. *see also* specific tribes
    American forces, 19, 21
    British forces, 21, 61
    fear of, 59
Inflexible (British ship), 29, 72
Iroquois, 15

Jersey Redoubt, 33–34
Johnson, Samuel, 79
Johnson, Thomas, 81–82

Kahnawake Mohawks, 51
Ketchum, Richard, 87, 92
Kimball, David, 90
Kinney, John, 41
Kosciuszko, Thaddeus, 55, *55*
    and Agrippa Hull, 21
    construction batteries, 61
    Delaware River caissons, 48, 55
    Enoch Poor portrait, *48*
    and Jeduthan Baldwin, 54

INDEX   101

map of Ticonderoga/Mount
    Independence, *71*
St. Clair court-martial, 75
Ticonderoga construction, 54

La Chute River, 78
Lacey, John, 39–40
Lake Champlain
    Abenaki sites, 15
    control of, 27–35
    map, *31*
    strategic waterway, 6
    Ticonderoga/Mount Independence
        narrows, *49, 50, 51*
Lake Champlain Maritime Museum, 27, 60
Lake George, 6, 7
    controlled by American, 35
    defense of, 53
    Diamond Island, 83
    Indian attack, 51
    supply route, 14, 27, 30, 62
Lake George Landing, 62, 77, 78
Lincoln, Benjamin, 75, 79
log boom
    blocks British, 35
    broken, 40
    contructed, 33
    cut by British, 71–72
    repaired, 52
Long, Pierce, 44
Lossing, Benson, 88
lotteries, 54
Loyal Convert (British gondola), 29
Lyon, Matthew, 87

Maguire, J. Robert, 90
Mahan, Alfred T., 36
malaria, 20
Manchester (Vermont), 74
Maria (British schooner), 29, *78, 79, 82*
Marshall, Thomas, 53
Masada, 91
Massachusetts troops, 17, 28, 34, 44, 53, 58, 69, 78–79
Massow, Frederika Charoltte Louise von. *see* Riedesel, Baroness
McLaughlin, Scott, 60
measles, 62
medicine vial (artifact), *20*

military engineering, 17–18
military roads, *7, 70*, 74. *see also* Crown Point; Mount Independence-Hubbardton
Mohawk River, 58, 63
Mohawks, 51
Mohicans, 21
Montcalm, Marquis de, 9
Montgomery, Richard, 5, *6*
Montresor, John, 7
Monument Hill (Hubbardton), *72*, 74
monuments, *44, 74, 84*, 88–89
mosquitoes, 20, 66, 72
Mount Defiance. *see also* Sugar Hill
    British defenses, 78
    plan to fortify, 48
    recaptured by Americans, 81
    view from, *64–65*
Mount Hope, 24, 62
Mount Independence
    American retreat from, 65–74
    American retreat to, 59, 61–62
    American siege of, 82
    burned, 85
    construction, American, 17–25
    construction, British, 78
    images
        across lake, *88*
        aerial, *4, 35*
        from Citadel, *23*
        Hunter, *68, 69*
        from Mount Defiance, *12, 64–65*
        to north, *vi–vii*
        Pell, *89*
    maps
        German, *2, 82*
        hiking trails, *93*
        Hudson/Champlain corridor, *7*
        Kosciuszko, *71*
        Lidar, *10*
        Michel Capitaine de Chesnoy, *viii*
        topographic, *14*
        Trumbull, *8, 19*
        Wintersmith, *49, 50*
    named, 1, 20
    nineteenth century, 88
    prehistory, 15
    prepares for attack, 61–62
    preservation, 89–92

    survey, 89
    twentieth century, 89–93
Mount Independence Association, 89, 90
Mount Independence Visitor Center, *86*, 87, *90, 93*
Mount Independence-Hubbardton military road
    American retreat, 69, 71, 72
    Burgoyne plans to cut, 62, 66
    maps, *7, 70*
    monument, *74*
    planned construction, 31
    twentieth century research, 89
munitions laboratory, 24, 61

National Historic Landmark, 90
Native American soldiers. *see* Indians
navy, American, 27, 28, *28*
Nelson, John, 44
New England troops, 18, 19
New Hampshire Grants, 79. *see also* Vermont
New Hampshire troops, 17, 19, 34, 44, 53, 62, 69, 78–79
New Jersey troops, 18, 40–41, 44
New York (American gondola), 43
New York troops, 18, 31, 51
Newell, Graham, 89, 91
nuclear power plant, 90

Onion River, 40
Orwell (Vermont), 92
Otter Creek, 74

passenger pigeons, 54
Paterson, John, 17, 19, 21, 40, 52
Peale, Charles Willson, 58
Pélissier, Christophe, 25
Pell, John H. G., 90
Pell, John Howland, 89
Pell, Sarah G. T., 89
Pell family, 88
Pennsylvania troops, 17, 18, 19, 27, 28, *38*, 39–40, 44
Peters, Richard, 40
Philadelphia (American gondola), *26*, 27, 36
Philadelphia II (replica gondola), 27
Pictorial Field-Book of the American Revolution (Lossing), 88
Pittsford Ridge, 74

Poor, Enoch, *48*
    Arthur St. Clair court-martial, 75
    defends Ticonderoga, 34
    ordered south, 40
    retreat, 69
Porter, Elisha, 22
powder horn (artifact), *22, 42*
Powell, H. Watson, 78, 81, 83, *83*, 84
power plants, 90
Pringle, Joel, 45
Putnam's Point, 62
putrid fever, 22

Québec, attacked, 5, *6*

rations. *see* diet
Rattlesnake Hill, 1, 18, 20
rattlesnakes, 17, 81
Reed, James, 19, 22, 34
reenactors, *72, 86, 91, 92, 93*
Reynolds, Joshua, *63*
Reynolds, Thomas, 89
Richelieu River, 6
Riedesel, Baroness, 45, *45*, 63, 80
Riedesel, Friedrich Adolf, 74, 80, *80*
Robbins, Ammi, 22
Robinson, David, 89
Royal George (British ship), 72
Royal Savage (American schooner), 31, 36
rum, 30, 43
Rupertinoe gun, 60
Rusco, David, 42
Rusco Powder Horn, 42, *42*
Rutland (Vermont), 31, 69, *70*, 74
Ryne, Timothy, 45

Sabbath Day Point, 51
Saratoga, Battles of, 74, 83
Saratoga National Historical Park, *84*
Schaick, Goose Van, 53
Schroder, Ernst, 81
Schröder, Johann Heinrich, *80*
Schuyler, Philip, 9, *9*
    background, 8–9
    court-martial, 74, 75
    on Crown Point troops, 9
    decision to fortify Mount Independence, 11, 12
    establishes shipyard, 27

    on fortifications, 48
    and Gates, 9, 48, 50, 53, 54
    on Mount Independence location, 5, 11, 13
    move from Crown Point, 14
    orders to St. Clair, 54, 58
    plans for Ticonderoga/Mount Independence, 9, 52–53
    on probabilty of attack, 61
    replaced by Gates, 74
    on retreat from Hubbardton, 74
    and St. Clair, 66
    St. Clair court-martial, 75
scurvy, 48
Second Brigade, 19, 92
Seth Warner Fife & Drum Corps, *92*
Shepardson, Zephaniah, *16, 17*, 19, 30
sickness. *see* disease
Skenesborough, *70*
    retreat to, 69–70, 71–72
    shipyard, 27–28
smallpox, 5–6, 22
snakes, 17, 81
soldiers (American)
    camp followers, 45
    daily life, *16, 17*, 30, 32, *38, 43*, 53–54
    diet, 29, 30, *30*, 40, 54
    housing, 19
    retreat from Ticonderoga/Mount Independence, 69–71
    winter, 39, 40–41, *41*, 43–44
soldiers (British), daily life, 78
Southern Battery, *62*, 92
Split Rock, 36
springs, 30
St. Clair, Arthur, *58, 75*
    agrees to abandon Ticonderoga, 59
    announces independence, 19–20
    background, 57
    command at Ticonderoga, 57
    commands Fourth Brigade, 19
    on condition of fortifications, 58
    court-martial, 74, 75
    decision to retreat, 66
    on defending Ticonderoga, 59
    disagrees with Schuyler, 66
    on Indian threat, 59
    on Mount Independence location, 47
    orders burning Lake George Landing, 62
    orders to fortify Mount Independence, 54, 58
    organizes retreat, 69–70
    post-Revolution career, 75
    on preparedness for attack, 57, 58
    prepares for British attack, 61–62
    recalled by Congress, 74
    reports to Schuyler, 9
    retreat, 74
    on retreat, 66–67
    size of force, 62
    on supplies, 58
St. Jean, Canada, 6
Staddard, N. Richardson, *88*
Star Fort, *24, 25*, 70, 71
Starbuck, David, 91–92
Stark, John, 13, 19, *19*, 40
Starke, John, 82
Stark's Point, 19
Stockbridge Indians, 21, *21*
Stockton, Richard, 47
Stoddard, N. Richardson, *88*
storehouses, 24
strong ground (quote), 5, 12, 14
Sugar Hill (Sugar Loaf), 48, 65–66. *see also* Mount Defiance
Sullivan, John, 12
survey, 89
sutlers, 30, 78

Tenent, William, 33
Thacher, James, 45, 71
The Great Warpath: British Military Sites from Albany to Crown Point (Starbuck), 91
The Mount Independence-Hubbardton 1776 Military Road (Wheeler), 89
Third Brigade, 19, 92
Three Mile Point, 33, 62
three-pronged attack, 63
Thunderer (British radeau), 29
Ticonderoga. *see* Fort Ticonderoga
Travels Through the Interior Parts of America (Anburey), *59*
Treatise of Military Discipline (Bland), 18
Truex Cullins & Partners, 90
Trumbull (American galley), 34–35
Trumbull, John
    attack of Quebec, *6*
    Burgoyne surrenders, *85*
    on disease, 20, 22
    explores Mount Independence, 11–12, 17
    Mount Independence map, *8, 19*
    portrait Schuyler, *9*
    portrait St. Clair, *75*
    on robbery, 11
    self-portrait, *8*
    on strength of fortifications, 34

Valcour Island, Battle of, 32, 36, *36*
    African American soldiers at, 21
    map, *37*
    Native Americans at, 21
Varick, Richard, 58, 59, 62
Vermont (state). *see also* New Hampshire Grants
    auction iron salvage, 87
    Division of Historic Preservation, 60
    Historic Sites Board, 89
    purchase of Mount Independence, 89
Vermont Electric Power Company (VELCO), 90
Vermont troops, 62, 78–79, 81, 84–85
Viereck, Ellen, *61, 78*
Viereck, Phillip, *61*

Wait, Benjamin, 84–85
Wait, Joseph, 22
Wallace, Richard, 79, *79*, 81
Walloomsack River, 78
Warner, Jonathan, 79, 82
Warner, Seth
    Battle of Bennington, 79, *84*
    Battle of Hubbardton, 72, 74
    regiment captured, 85
Washington (American row-galley), *26*, 27
Washington, George, 13–14, 58, 65, 74
Wasmus, Julius Friedrich, 71
Wayne, Anthony, *40*
    assigned command, 39
    on camp followers, 45
    on cold, 43
    on condition of troops, 43, 44
    discipline, 41, 43
    explores Mount Independence, 17
    on food supplies, 30
    frustrations of command, 40
    Gates on, 40
    on imminent British attack, 51
    John Lacey on, 39
    leaves Ticonderoga/Mount Independence, 52
    reports to Schuyler, 9
    on troop departures, 44
Webster, Samuel, 79, *79*
Wells, Bayze, 17
Wheeler, Joseph L., 89
Wheeler, Mabel A., 89
Whitcomb, Benjamin, 59, 61
wicket (ball game), *16*, 17
Wilkinson, James, 36
William, Frederick, Baron de Woedtke, 12
Williams, John A., 89
Wilson, James, 58
wine, 43
wine bottle (artifact), *43*
Winooski River, 40
winter, 39–44, *41*
Wintersmith, Charles, 48, *49*, 50
women, 30, 45, 78
Wood, Joseph, 41
Worthen, Ezekiel, 44
Wynkoop, Cornelius, 11, 31
Wynkoop, Jacobus, 31

yellow fever, 20, 22

Zaboly, Gary
    Americans attack Mount Independence, *76*
    camp followers, *45*
    daily life of troops, *16*
    fortifications await British attack, *34*
    Great Bridge construction, *46*
    soldiers in winter, *38*
    view from Mount Independence, *vi–vii*

Ernest Haas, *Mount Independence 1776-1777 / Mount Independence Coalition*

The Mount Independence Coalition

Mount Independence State Historic Site in Orwell, Vermont, is administered by the Vermont Division for Historic Preservation. The Mount Independence Coalition is a nonprofit organization run by volunteers and supported by its membership. A Memorandum of Understanding with the Division defines the relationship between the two entities:

The Vermont Division for Historic Preservation and the Mount Independence Coalition cooperate with, and respect and enhance the efforts of, one another to preserve the historic and natural integrity of the Mount, and to increase its accessibility to the public.

At the time *Strong Ground* is being published, the Mount Independence Coalition will have been in existence for almost three decades. The Coalition has been the beneficiary of the support and work of a passionate membership, including former board members who gave so much of their time and effort to fulfilling the ideals set forth in the Memorandum. Space does not permit thanking everyone who deserves our appreciation, but we want to especially acknowledge two exceptional past leaders of our organization. As an early crusader for a book about the Mount, David Pinkham played a key role in making *Strong Ground* a reality. The commitment Louise Ransom brought to her years as leader of the Coalition has given us the wherewithal to be able to publish *Strong Ground*, and provides the solid foundation on which the Coalition rests today. We salute David and Louise and everyone who has helped the Coalition reach this important milestone in its existence.

Support the Coalition.
Support Mount Independence.

If you would like to help the Coalition continue its necessary work, please consider becoming a member or making a donation. Learn how at our organization's website: www.mountindependence.org.

Thank you for reading *Strong Ground*. Spread the word.

— *The board of the Mount Independence Coalition*

Steve Zeoli, President *Ennis Duling*
Jim Ross, Vice President *R. Duncan Mathewson, III*
Bill Dick, Treasurer *Rustan Swenson*
Ron Morgan, Secretary *Joe Taparauskas*
Mark Brownell